# Bark Like a Dog!

*Outrageous Ideas for Actors*

## Herb Parker

Spring Knoll Press

Cover Art by Herb Parker

Edited by Delbert Hall

ISBN-13: 978-0615866574

ISBN-10: 0615866573

Printed in the United States of America

For my brother

Harold

And in memory of our sister,

Pat

...For anything so o're done is from the purpose of playing, whose end, both at the first and now, was and is, to hold as 'twere the mirror up to nature; to show virtue her feature, scorn her own image, and the very age and body of the time his form and pressure.

*Hamlet*

# CONTENTS

# Acknowledgments

I would like to thank friends and colleagues who helped me greatly in the writing of this book; Ms. Emily Landham; from East Tennessee State University, Professors Karen Brewster, Bobby Funk, Cara Harker and Dr. Katherine Weiss; Dr. Delbert Hall of Spring Knoll Press; Eric Peterson, Producing Artistic Director, Oldcastle Theatre Company; From the College of William and Mary, Professor Christopher Owens, Producing Artistic Director, Virginia Shakespeare Festival and Barry P. Katz, Theatrical Agent, Dulcina Eisen Associates, New York, New York. Dear Friends all. Thank you so much.

Finally, I want to thank all of my students. You have challenged me, enlightened me, sometimes even exasperated me but most of all you have inspired me, and you are the reason I wanted to write this book. You have taught me how to teach—or at least how to *aspire* to teach—and for that I am forever grateful.

# Introduction

Welcome, hither,
As is the spring to th' earth.

*The Winter's Tale*

*Bark Like a Dog!* came out of a workshop I conducted at the Southeastern Theatre Conference's 64th Annual Convention in March of 2013. I came up with the name for it out of a desire to do two things: 1: To produce a snazzy, catchy title which might hopefully catch the eye and cause young actors to attend, and, more importantly, 2: To help these actors make bigger, bolder, more risky choices in their acting and auditioning. In all my years of teaching this has been my number one challenge with acting students; they all shy away from making the "Big Choice." They hesitate and mumble that they don't want to 'do too much,' they are concerned about 'going over the top.' It seems that no matter how much I encourage them, plead with them to go further, to do *too much*, they manage to hang on to what is perceived to be the be-all end-all response to the question of a big choice: "Less is More." Even though, with all due respect to these young folks, they are at that moment a far cry from even being close to be prompted to do 'less.' It is as if they are possessed of some unshakable fear of being wrong, or at least of not being *right*; of being thought silly and made to look ridiculous in front of their peers who of course are frightened of the same things they are. At the bottom of this confusion I suspect is the fear that plagues so many of us who pursue a career as an actor; the fear of being exposed as not having *any talent*. It always tugs at my heartstrings when thinking about it: "Do you think I'm any good?" they ask after performing an exercise, not so much with words as with their eyes. I was once one of them, many years ago, asking that same question of my own teachers. I am pleased to report that my own fear was answered with a 30-year career as an actor in regional theatre. While I cannot guarantee this for you, I do hope I can at least help you in the classroom as you wrestle with that 'big choice.'

Much of what I am about to say is not really new; we know that drama is created out of conflict. Without that conflict there can be no play of any kind. So while I do not seek to re-invent the wheel what I would like to do is at least *add to it*, and I hope to do so by proposing this: a play—*every* play, no matter what the genre, is about an *outrageous situation*. And taking this thought a step further, it makes sense to me that human beings caught up in an outrageous situation will require means *just as outrageous* to deal with it.

When fully embraced by a young actor—*you*—I am convinced that this simple understanding can help you overcome your fears and make bigger choices. Not only that, when properly applied it can be the source of even greater choices from your *own* experience, your own impulse and talent. Your work will be enriched and who knows? You just might even become more hirable as an actor.

This book is divided into two parts, the first devoted to scene work and the second to preparing monologues for audition, both guided by this idea of the outrageous. My approach in the book is as if I am speaking to you in class, as if you have just done a scene or a monologue or have asked questions about someone else doing a scene or monologue. My assumption is that you are new to the study of acting, but I hope that you will be able to benefit from it even if you have been studying and working for some time. In the voices of my "students" here I hope you will find yourself somewhere and that perhaps I will be answering questions you may have once had. My 'technique' for acting and actor training is of course based on the teachings of Konstantin Stanislavski, but what's more it is an amalgam of every teacher I have ever had, gussied up into a veritable meat loaf which I now call my own. I hope your own technique will become the same for you as well because I want you to study with as many teachers as you can, act for as many directors as can cast you and talk shop with as many acting colleagues as possible—this will become your real classroom, this is the way you will truly learn. Some of these ideas you probably have heard before ('Less is more,' 'Try Not to Cry,' 'Act on the Line,' to name a few). I think that is as it should be. A good idea sooner or later becomes everybody's idea; we actors pass along from generation to generation what makes sense as we learn and grow. You will also realize soon enough that I repeat myself—as I do in my classroom—please excuse me; the repetitiveness comes out of my own energy and passion and also out of my realization that what works for scene study can also work for monologue study, as well.

I hope that you will thumb through at least parts of this book constantly, that it will become dog-eared, the spine broken from being jammed into your back pocket, maybe as you stand in line waiting to go in to audition or interview with an agent. I want this to become a resource for you—as every other experience of your young life will be a resource for you—as you continue that actor's life-long journey: To 'hold the mirror up to nature.'

Good fortune attend your endeavors!

Herb Parker

# Part One: Working on Scenes

"We will meet; and there we may rehearse most obscenely, and courageously."

*A Midsummer Night's Dream*

# 1. Love and Outrage

**Love**  \ˈləv\ *n*
1 *a (1)*: strong affection for another arising out of kinship or personal ties *(2)*: attraction based on sexual desire: affection and tenderness felt by lovers *(3)*: affection based on admiration, benevolence, or common interests
   *b*: an assurance of affection

**Out·ra·geous**  \(ˌ)aut-ˈrā-jəs\  *adj*
1 *a* : exceeding the limits of what is usual
   *b* : not conventional or matter-of-fact : FANTASTIC

*Webster's New Collegiate Dictionary, 1977*

For our work over the course of these pages that follow I would like for us to agree on something. I consider it very important, important enough to be nearly sacred, in its depth towering enough to be almost Dionysian, and ultimately profound enough to be never far from the heart of anyone who has ever had the dream in their soul of being an actor on the stage. At the risk of sounding overly lofty, I believe that in embracing this idea your acting will be infused with greater imagination and power as you go forth in your career. The notion is this:

## A Play is about Human Beings caught in an Outrageous Situation, Caused by *Love*

I want you to accept this premise for our work. *A play is about human beings caught in an outrageous situation, caused by Love.* This is what makes for its conflict, and its joy. If any of a plays' circumstance can be accepted as commonplace, routine or humdrum I say that it is not a worthy play to be done, least of all for the actor seeking to 'hold the mirror up to nature.' I believe this to be true of *every* great play, no matter how loud and theatrical or how subdued and understated; whether Absurdist or melodrama, farce or Slice of Life; Shakespeare or Sondheim, Euripides or Mamet, even Wilson or Chekhov. I submit that every play is about human beings struggling with this seemingly contradictory circumstance.

Do you think plays are not outrageous? That they can exist without love? Let me offer you a few examples from plays you undoubtedly have heard of, among the greatest ever written: a young Verona man drunk with love for the illusive Rosaline sneaks to a party at the home of the family which is at war with his family, and that very night meets the daughter of his sworn enemy and both of them fall immediately into everlasting love. Would you be willing to say this is out of the ordinary? Might it be possible to say it is *outrageous?* How about this one: a king discovers that an ancient prophesy that warned he would one day murder his father and marry his mother is true—and for good measure throw in the fact that he has had children by her! In horror his wife and mother hangs herself in the palace and he then gouges out his own eyes with her brooch. Cannot this be called outrageous—just perhaps? What do you think of this one: during World War II in the South Pacific a young woman from Arkansas falls in love with a French expatriate, a love so profound both he and she are moved to *sing* to one another about "Some Enchanted Evening." Later she has decided that she cannot love him and with the help of her fellow WAVES she declares in song that she is going to "Wash That Man Right out of My Hair." Such goings-on must be considered 'not conventional or matter-of-fact!' How about this one: a beautiful but inexperienced young girl in a small Kansas town meets a gruff, handsome young rake in her front yard on a Labor Day morning and exactly twenty-four hours later she is leaving the only home she has ever known to meet him in Tulsa, Oklahoma! Does not this 'exceed the limits of what is *usual?*' Or this one: two devoted friends meet each day, at the same hour, at the same place, waiting at long last for a third friend who has long promised to join them, who by plays' end has not appeared. The only word of him is brought by a messenger boy who assures the two waiting men that their missing friend will, *without fail,* come by tomorrow!

*Or lastly this: a throng of total strangers seat themselves in a darkened theater. They are there to sit and watch a group of even stranger people on a stage, wearing wild costumes and garish face paint, spewing forth memorized words. The garishly made-up people do this for two or three hours and, yes, for the balance of that duration the audience agrees to 'suspend their disbelief' and accept the live goings-on as **believable!***

Don't let the words 'outrageous' and 'love' fool you. I do not mean that a play is about yelling your guts out for three hours nor is it about mumbling unintelligibly with your back to the audience for four—that is not even required in *Medea.* I make the case that plays happen when you the actor are swept up in a maelstrom you have never dreamed of, so earth-shaking you do not know how to deal with it—yet, of course, you *must* deal with it. This is what constitutes the world in which characters live and propels every monologue they are forced to speak, and looking at it this way helps actors reach greater heights in their acting.

The "outrageous" I want you to embrace can be for *good* as well as *bad,* the love can be false as well as true. The characters can just as well be struggling to handle a tumult of *happiness* as well as sorrow. As quoted above, *Outrageous* merely means, "Exceeding the limits of what is usual," "not conventional or matter-of-fact," "fantastic," "unrestrained." *Love* on the other hand is defined as "strong affection for another arising out of kinship or personal ties," "attraction based on sexual desire," "warm attachment, enthusiasm, or devotion." I choose the term *outrageous* to describe the conflict inherent in every play because these definitions go even further than 'conflict,' and I choose to name *love* as the cause of the outrageous situation because love is the one thing that every human being searches for, longs for, fights and dies for. Whether for country or an idea or a single soul love is the life experience humankind so struggles to understand, yet begs so shamelessly to for favor. Love is the language every human being can understand by virtue of the fact that they *are* human beings, even if they might be separated by spoken language or culture. Greek Tragedy first and foremost is about the complicated, adversarial relationship between man and the gods. In speaking about these gods, Shakespeare said, 'they kill us for their sport.' Love is no less powerful, is no less omnipotent; at every turn it tosses us about like flies and on a whim can choose to shower us with accolades or condemn us to despair. In all of the examples I just mentioned, was not love at the center? Was not love arguably the cause? Romeo and Juliet, Oedipus and Jocasta, Nellie Forbush and Emile de Becque in *South Pacific*, Hal and Madge in William Inge's play *Picnic*, Vladimir and Estragon while *Waiting for Godot* and even, yes, the Actor and the Audience?

Young actor, the conflict that is outrageous for good or ill, the love that drives the human heart, these things which make the best of the drama possible are also what will help you improve your work so that you can get a job and 'hold the mirror up to nature' when you are cast in a play. Please bear with me and accept this notion as a guidepost as you prepare your scene work in class or your monologue for audition. In both cases it will serve the play, your work and your career. That is what I hope to help you with in this little book.

# 2. Outrageous? *Really?*

Though this be madness, yet there is method in't.

*Hamlet*

So, for an actor working on a scene or a monologue for audition, when I ask you to make choices that are 'outrageous' what do I mean? Earlier I cited Webster with definitions such as "exceeding the limits of what is usual," "unrestrained," and "fantastic." It is this that I am asking of the actor: to show no restraint, to do something unusual, perform that which is unbelievable (fantastic). Such 'outrageous' action is only to be expected from a character in the midst of an outrageous, love-driven situation – which is, we have already agreed, the world of a play!

But this kind of behavior does not always come easily for the actor in the sometimes intimidating confines of the classroom, so I have come up with exercises you can do, and it is no mistake that the word I choose to emphasize is *do*.

To help you I have listed below specific actions for you to choose from as you seek the outrageous to enliven your scene or monologue. I have tried as much as possible to limit the list to actions which can be done rather than thought about, and because they do not rely on the logical—that is, by their very nature they will come at the wrong place at the wrong time in order to 'exceed the limits of what is usual,'—you can do them anytime during the course of your monologue or scene and as often as you like. At the end of the list you will also see that I have included Rudolf

Laban's 8 Movement Analysis Efforts,[1] quite helpful in coming up with a range of movement or gesture for actors as well as dancers. You can mix them up and try a couple of them together at a time.

Use the list like this: rehearse either a monologue or a scene with another actor and during the scene—you decide when—pick one of these actions and throw it into the scene. In the middle of working on a monologue of Hamlet, for instance, how about suddenly barking like a dog? Or dancing an Irish jig? Or hop on one foot. *Just do it.* Why? Because we humans are flawed, unpredictable, unreliable creatures capable of doing *anything* if pushed far enough, even and especially if we would never *normally* do such things. Have you ever snapped at someone harshly, only to later rush to apologize, saying, "I am so sorry! That isn't like me at all!" Oh but it is! *It is,* my friends. What's more it is *alright* that it is! Because we are, as Prospero says, 'such stuff as dreams are made on.'

That is the method in this madness. These actions when used as a tool of exploration can lead the actor toward greater openness, more lively imagination and just perhaps, eventually, the *greater* choice more suitable to the scene and context of the play. Think of these actions as ripping on the pull cord to start the lawnmower; you are, in effect, jump starting your own imagination with reckless, weird, glorious actions in order to eventually find more *appropriate* actions that will serve you even better on stage and in the audition room. You are getting that much closer to making the big choice that so eludes actors just starting out in their training. You are learning to swim; come on in, the water's fine!

---

[1] Rudolf Laban with F.C. Lawrence, *Effort: Economy of Human Movement* London: MacDonald and Evans. 1947. (4th reprint 1967) **Rudolf von Laban** aka **Rudolf Laban** (1879 –1958) was a dance artist and theorist, notable as one of the pioneers of modern dance in Europe. His work laid the foundations for Laban Movement Analysis, Labanotation (Kinetography Laban), other more specific developments in dance notation and the evolution of many varieties of Laban Movement Study.

Here is the list, which includes sounds as well as physical actions:

*Herb's List of Outrageous Acts for your Scene or Monologue*

| | |
|---|---|
| Bark like a Dog | Eat like a mouse |
| Dance a jig | Eat like a squirrel |
| Dance an Irish Jig | Eat like a goat |
| Dance a polka | Eat like Cookie Monster |
| Dance a ballet | Make a Drinking Sound |
| Do a pirouette | Make a Swallowing Sound |
| Do a split like James Brown | Long Sigh after a Swallow |
| Do a cartwheel | Smack your lips |
| Hop Double Dutch | Throw a football |
| Hop on One Foot | Run with a football |
| Quack like a Duck | Avoid Imaginary tacklers |
| Walk like a Duck | Shoot a gun with your fingers |
| Gobble like a Turkey | Make a gunshot sound |
| Cluck like a Chicken | Make an explosion sound |
| Fly like a plane | Make a Mushroom cloud sound |
| Duck from a grenade | Make a drowning sound |
| Fall on bended knee | Make a gurgling sound |
| Fall down on both knees | Make a baby sound |
| Fall on hands and knees | Make a monkey sound |
| Beg like a dog | Stalk like a buzzard |

Pant like a dog

Howl like a dog

Howl like a wolf

Meow like a cat

Gallop like a horse

"Argh!" like a Pirate

Shoot like a Slingshot

Swim on the floor like a Fish

Fall flat on your back

Fry like bacon on your back

Walk like the opposite sex

Purr like a cat

Chirp like a bird

Make a car engine sound

Start a car with your voice

Snake across the floor

Start a lawn mower with your body / voice

## Laban's 8 Efforts

| Glide | Flick | Push | Punch |
|-------|-------|------|-------|
| Float | Dab | Slash | Wring |

These are only a few choices. Try to add some of your own and see what sudden acts you might find even more outrageous. Also as you perform them remember that they can be realized sensually as well as literally. For instance, if you have chosen to use "Snake across the floor" for a monologue of, say, Mosca from *Volpone* or Iago from *Othello* (or even Lady Macbeth), you can either get onto your belly on the floor, drawing your butt up into the air, your chin and knees on the floor and proceed to propel yourself forward like the actual reptile or you may just as easily translate the physical *suggestion* of "snake across a floor" into the human movements and gestures of your character while speaking (such as quick, snatching, tongue-darting). Try them both ways. Though it is my hope that these actions will spark more exciting relationship values between characters in the scene they are also quite useful in finding specific character *traits,* such as how to walk, talk and gesture with the hands.

At first the idea is to make choices that are as far from the *reality of the play as possible.* You are in effect performing a script-based improvisation that will loosen you up. Eventually, as you get more used to doing it, you can scale down your choices and your 'outrageous' actions can be more closely related to the organic given circumstances of the scene. Let us say your character is holding a handbag when the scene begins. You can choose to throw it at your partner, or slap at them with it or empty it over their head or onto *your own* head. If the two of you are sitting on chairs, you can climb up and stand on your own chair or you can leap up and kick it over. These fantastic choices will even further connect you to the needs of the characters, sparking compelling ideas that will not only lead to a more interesting relationship in the scene, but probably—if your partner is truly listening to you and taking what you are *giving*—produce equally big choices from your partner, as well.

# 3. The First Question You Must Ask

Study what you most affect.

*Taming of the Shrew*

You have been cast in a scene by your acting teacher. When working on a role for a scene the first question you must always ask is, "What Do I Want?" You must also remember that your character is caught up in the midst of an outrageous situation, caused by love, and you must fight your way out of it.

What do I mean by this? *Fight your way out of it.* The word *fight* is intentional. Fight. Imagine that you are forced up against a wall and unbelievable calamity—or unbelievable *joy*—is coming at you. What would you do? This is what your scene is "about." It is, in my view, the best way to employ Stanislavski's "Magic If."[2] Your scene **partner** is that coming calamity, **they** have forced you up against the wall, and it is toward **them** that you must flail your fists or shower your kisses. If in fact you have been placed in the position of having to fight for your life or wield unimaginable joy, what thoughts might come to your mind? Let us explore the possibilities, and realize that there are many of them and they are the same whether the outrage is tragic or joyous:

---

[2] Konstantin Stanislavski, *An Actor Prepares* New York: Theatre Arts Books. 1936. (23rd reprint 1969) 31. Stanislavski (1863-1938) was a renowned Russian Actor Director Teacher best known for his system of acting which became known in America as "The Method."

1. What can you *do*? Or *make* the force outside of you do? What *weapons* are at your disposal to defend or ingratiate yourself?
2. What *obstacles*—real or imagined—stand in your way?

If you look on your scene as happening in bounds which you accept as unbelievable and amazing in their craziness, eventually you will be compelled to think thoughts just as crazy and unbelievable in order to survive. The choices at your disposal must *match the height* of your challenge. This should still be your attitude even if your scene, on the face of it, entails nothing more than a conversation between two people.

Then there is the question of love being at the center of the scene. Think of how outrageous the circumstances are between Toozenbach and Irina in Anton Chekhov's *The Three Sisters*. In the last act of the play, the woefully ugly Toozenbach is saying good-bye to his new bride Irina before going off to be shot to death; foolishly he has accepted a duel with Solyony and on the way he passes a brief, and final, moment with Irina. At one point, in calling out to her, he turns, perhaps hoping against all hope that she *might* answer, "What, darling?" But the moment never comes, she only replies, "What?" and as Chekhov says in the stage directions, *not knowing what to say,* he replies: "I haven't had my coffee this morning. Could you have them make some for me?" Always: the outrage need not entail bombastic violence in word or deed. It simply must seek to scratch the surface of the bottomless depth that is the human heart.

## *Getting Started on Your Scene*

To prepare your scene you must:

1. Read the play from beginning to end. Allow yourself to simply get into the story; try to imagine that you are in the audience watching it being performed and allow it to affect you emotionally, just as it would any theatergoer. Read the play over again, as many times as necessary, to get a sense

of what it might be about; how does the playwright employ events as tools to tell his or her story?

2. You must canvass the script for *every* instance of 3 things:
   A. What the **playwright** says about you in the stage directions.
   B. What the playwright has **other characters** say about you in the play.
   C. What the playwright has **you say about yourself**.

3. You must know everything that happens in the play *before, leading up to and including* your scene. What you are looking for is everything the playwright has placed in the play that will inform and foreshadow the events of your scene. Once you have accumulated all of the early scenes in the play that at least reference your character you must then create a bulleted list. Consider this a "cheat sheet" you can refer back to as you work on your scene.

4. As you continue to study your character, what you say and do, you must never make value judgments of any kind, such as, "Boy is he weird! This gal is crazy! What an *awful* person!" There is no harm in being aware *intellectually* that the playwright may have decided that a certain character is a 'good guy' or a 'bad guy,' but such observations based on *qualities* are of no use to you as you work on the part. You must never play a bad guy to "show the audience what happens to bad guys!" That is preaching a sermon. Your job is to present a complex, compelling portrayal of a flawed human being. It is the *audience's* job to decide if you are "good," or "bad."

5. Your empathy for your character must be absolute. You must accept everything that your character does as that which he or she *had* to do in order to survive in the world the playwright has created. This does not mean that you are blind to them doing wrong; rather you forgive them and rationalize their bad actions as necessary to survive,

especially if they are wrong. Admit it; would not *you* do this in your own life?

6.  You will need to provide simple blocking (movement) to your scene. Do not stress out about it; think of blocking as movement with *motivation;* try to work out with your partner exactly where in the text it appears either they or you are getting too close, pushing too hard, sufficient to cause one of you to have to move away from the other to catch your breath (it may even be that the playwright will have written it into the stage directions). Unless stage combat is required in the scene a lot of blocking is not required; keep it simple and concentrate on fighting for what you want from the other actor.

What will help both of you is if, in your early rehearsals, you work on the scene simply sitting down. Concentrate on looking at the other person and do not look away; in fact, try your best to keep on looking until, somehow, you are subconsciously *forced* to look away, or you force them to do so. This will lead you toward the moment in the scene when either of you must get up, due either to action played or action thwarted, and move away. This will constitute 'blocking' that is motivated and organic. Hopefully your partner will be so in tune with what you are 'giving' them that they will be moved to get up and follow you either to rub in the success of their objective or change tactics in order to make peace with you. In any event the scene should not require much in the way of physical movement; the action should be more about what the two of you want from each other than how often you both move.

7.  You must look in the script for chances to play the *opposites* in your character. In Shakespeare we call this *antithesis.* In order for a character to seem real and fully realized as a flawed human being they must be able to perform what is genuinely *contradictory* about them. One

way, as Shakespeare's characters do, is to constantly compare opposites; hot and cold, life and death, day versus night, fat over thin, etc. This helps the character as well as the audience to always be aware of *both sides* of an issue, both sides of the human heart. It prevents us from just saying, "Well this is a bad guy, period!" Life in William Shakespeare's work—as well as all great plays— is much more complex than that. Unless you are acting in Melodrama, no hero or heroine is all good or villain or villainess all bad; they simply, like you and me, are fighting for their life and those they love in an outrageous world. The playwright may well have decided who is good or bad but you as the actor must present to the audience a character with a depth as great as their own; let the audience root for whom they choose and hate whom they despise. You, as an exciting, dangerous actor, will make your own indiscriminate choices, whether you are playing Adolf Hitler or Little Bo Peep.

8. Last, but not least, you must find the Love in your play. Is it requited? Refused? Lost? Longed-for? Imagined? *Where is the love?* If the play is at all worth doing, it will be there.

# 4. Scoring: Writing Down the Palpitations of the Human Heart

O, sir, I will not be so hard-hearted. I will give out divers schedules of my beauty. It shall be inventoried, and every particle and utensil labeled to my will.

*Twelfth Night*

My words fly up, my thoughts remain below.
Words without thoughts never to heaven go.

*Hamlet*

You already have in Chapter 2 a list of outrageous actions you can inject into your scene or speech. You will also find in Appendix B a simple chart that may be useful when you list possible choices to try when playing your scene. Below in Figure 1 is an example of it:

| YOUR CHARACTER NAME | SUPER OBJECTIVE | OBJECTIVE | ACTION | OBSTACLE |
|---|---|---|---|---|
|  |  |  |  |  |

Fig.1. Actor's Character Score Sheet.

What you do is take all you have learned from carefully reading the script and record it in the space provided, or use a suitable chart of your own making. In script analysis for actors this is what we call *Scoring*. It is your interpretation, graphically, of what your character wants in life (the super-objective), in each individual scene (objective), what you do to get it (action via active verb) and what stands in your way of getting it (obstacle). Admittedly doing such a thing is folly, for it is attempting to blue print and organize human action. Crazy, yes? Not conventional or matter of fact, right? But in rehearsal with your partner it can be very helpful as a psychological support of the given circumstances in the play. This 'score' is meant to include cast-off attempts as well as final decisions; therefore it records your whole course of trial and error. This is valuable as you dig into your imagination for the best, most outrageous loving choice that fits the outrageous loving situations of the play your character has been placed in.

This score is not meant however to be played when you actually do the scene. That moment must be reserved for when you finally get up to play the scene as rehearsed—that is, *perform*. The blue print of your score is only meant to inform your artistic instincts as you study by yourself; it is *homework*.

Below is what to record in your Actors' Score:

## Super-objective

Stanislavski's notion of the Super-objective is more akin to the theme of the play. These days when we speak of super-objective we normally mean the character's lifetime goal or aspiration but for the actor's purpose I like for us to speak of it as the *life of the play* during the ensuing acts, only what the playwright has given us. It does no harm to your work if you speculate about what might have happened to your character after the play ends, but it is of no use to you in actually getting on stage. All that you can reasonably play is what is in the script; the script is the story, period. On the other hand the super-objective is a through-line for your character, your reason for being, what holds you together (also called the *spine*) and as such it can be and should be broad enough to encompass your entire life the audience sees during the evening at the theater. It can be stated very simply, such as, "I must avenge my father's murder" (*Hamlet*) or, "I must get Brick to have sex with me again" (Maggie in *Cat on a Hot Tin Roof*) or, "I must save the people of Thebes by finding Laos' Killer" (*Oedipus*) or "I must get my daughter Laura married" (Amanda in *The Glass Menagerie*). It must be sufficiently broad to cover their entire life we see or hear about in the play.

# Objective

Unlike the Super-objective that must cover a character's needs for the entire play, the Objective is what you want on a scene-by-scene basis. Not what you do to get it, but what you want to get as a *result* of what you do. It is behind all of the actions you perform during the course of a scene and throughout the entire play and it can change mid-scene, depending upon how your scene partner is responding to you (also called what they are 'giving' you. They are giving you what they are giving you based on what the playwright has told *them* to do, too!). Objective has also been called Intention and Action. Consider a character's evening of scene by scene objectives as building blocks which, stacked up by the play's end, will help them get what they want for the life of the play. Just realize that the blocks are not even or without disruption; along the way it will be necessary to adjust them as circumstances demand. Your character will need to occasionally change their desires (objectives); they will need to take a *beat*. A Beat is when you change your objective or your action. This happens when you must change course mid-stream because your scene partner has not given you what you want. Some directors use the term *Step* to refer to this.

# Action

Simplest put, this is what you do to get what you want. You are putting a name to your actions. It matters tremendously how explicit a term—*an active verb*—you choose to describe what you are doing; it will be in direct proportion to how hard—and how outrageously—you fight for your objective. An example:

Joe wants Bob to loan him $20. So Joe asks his friend, "Bob, can you loan me $20?" What might be the *best* choice of active verb Joe could use to obtain his objective of getting Bob to loan him $20?

To convince

To praise

To suck up (to)

To accuse

To polish (as in an apple)

To plead

To grovel (as on the floor)

To kiss (as in butt)

What do you think would work best? That is, which of the choices above might cause Joe to go after Bob with *greater commitment?* To compel Joe to *need* Bob more in the scene?

The answer is that a lot depends on that active verb.

Any of the choices listed above are good active verbs for Joe, but of course there are many possibilities. How about *"Grovel"?* It suggests not only that you do something, it describes *how* you do it; sensually the actor can be drawn to an image of physically rooting around in the dirt below, bowing their head in supplication; such a word evokes someone who is more likely to reach out and touch the other person on stage, to look them straight in the eyes, to raise their voice, to knead their hair, to reach out and grab their partner by the ankle if necessary. Any image which *incites action* is a good one; this is how choice of an active verb works at its best. In playing an action your emotions are ultimately going to be engaged because of how strong and extreme your choice is. Playing actions the way they ought to be played is hard work, work causes you to exert yourself, exerting yourself causes heat, heat causes you to tire and being tired leads to frustration. This is how to begin the process of playing emotion on stage. Your scene partner will have to come up with a reply to your action *just as outrageous as you gave them.* When your two actions meet— *bam!*—We have a thrilling evening in the theatre; that is, we have a *play.* There is a diagram to this effect later in this chapter.

## Obstacle

This is what stands in your way, what is preventing you from getting your objective and what makes it necessary for you to change your actions. It is the invisible brick wall that stands between you and what you want most in the scene, be it in a single moment, during the act, or for the entire course of the play. An Obstacle can be an actual person or persons, a set of circumstances or supernatural forces; it is all up to the playwright. It can even be *you.* For Hamlet it can be the Ghost of his father, the horrific sight of his Uncle and Mother in wedlock, or even Hamlet himself. However if you should decide that you yourself are the obstacle just don't allow your performance to become *introverted;* you are always fighting for something that is *outside* of you, eluding you, taunting you.

## Excite Us! The Verb You Choose *Matters*

This is what acting is. It is true that the ultimate, intended result of the actors' toil is emotion, but in my opinion the only way to get there with consistency—that is, the way a *professional* does it—is through at least some form of Stanislavski's system of Physical Actions.[3] Emphasize the word *action.* It is perfectly all right, in the study and reading of your play, scene and monologue, to take

---

[3] Ibid. Chapter 3, "Action."

note of the emotions which must result between the audience and the actor—but you must never seek these emotions directly: they are not reliable enough. You can only reach them, grasp at them, claw for them through the playing of an action to obtain an objective. You must *do* something, and if that first choice does not succeed you must try something else and then something else and then something else. This is the process that Stanislavski believed would aid the actor in eventually tapping into their subconscious. It is also the most professional way to work: you can fight for an objective by playing an action whether that day you feel like doing it or not, for eight performances a week whether you feel like it or not. Fighting with an active verb as your weapon can be done over and over again, it is not bound by 'feeling it' or by 'inspiration.' Young actor, the farther you go in this business the more you will realize that it is not about the 'stars in your eyes,' it is about the *'perspiration on your brow.'* In scoring your script you are seeking to codify technically what flesh and blood human beings do every single day of their lives; they live and interact with their fellow men and women. This is because in the work-a-day world we probably have some knowledge of the person we are dealing with; we may not be aware of what they are keeping from us but we know for the most part who they are and what we want from them and what the rules of engagement with them are—we know the *given circumstances.* But these actions are *intuitive;* people seek love or revenge in the world in which they live without once thinking, "Now what Action should I Play as I approach this Task?" To do so would be to act like a robot. I repeat: this work is not meant to hem you in—it is meant to *unleash your imagination.* I tell my students that if you can produce a believable performance without doing all of this scoring, then don't bother with it! Scoring is only for those moments when a particularly challenging role might cause you to think, "What is going on in this person's head? I just can't figure it out!" That is when I hope you will turn to scoring the script. It is about getting your engine started; how you drive the car is your business.

## Playing Emotion is Doing, *Not* Feeling

Emotion by its nature is not very reliable. It is too quick, too sudden, and too reliant upon the mystery that is the human heart. We just don't know where emotion or feelings come from; we do know *that* we feel, that we experience love and hate and everything in between. But these feelings are by no means under our control—quite the contrary. It is not reliable for an actor to consciously try to show emotion because such an enterprise cannot be sustained; it might be possible to conjure it up one night, and maybe even another night, and another. But indefinitely? After, say, thirty nights? Or a hundred nights? How many? How might you measure such an attempt? By the number of tears generated? How many tears, then? One? Two? Three? By the trickle or the stream? Even if it were possible to 'show' emotion to an audience, it would certainly change from night to night, because we flesh and blood creatures are different every night, our blood pressure is different, our life off stage is different, the weather outside is different, that very day is different. That is why when an actor attempts directly to show emotion it is usually either a miserable failure or a short-lived series of hit and miss. Nor is it helpful—out of a laudable attempt to be 'professional'—for the actor to *indicate* the desired emotion either; that is, to grossly imitate to the audience the *result* of an action played without having actually played the action. Consider the actress playing Masha in *The Three Sisters*, faced with Chekhov's Act Four stage direction, *"Masha weeps violently."* To pretend this moment on one hand might technically satisfy the job of the actor but it falls short in honesty; the audience may not have the language of the theatre to judge such things but they just might utter, "There was something wrong in that last scene. I just didn't *believe* Masha's acting!"

Yet, the actor's great challenge is to *repeat* a performance night after night whether they feel like doing it or not, because it is their *job* to do so. So what is the performer to do? How do you get emotionally where the playwright has destined you to go? The answer is you play an action against an obstacle in order to get your objective.

Below in Fig. 2 is a diagram that tries to track the means by which actors create emotion. It is an indirect route, as you can see. When your actions collide with an obstacle—such as the actions played by *another* actor—the resulting generated "friction" will be genuine human feeling—i.e., *emotion.*

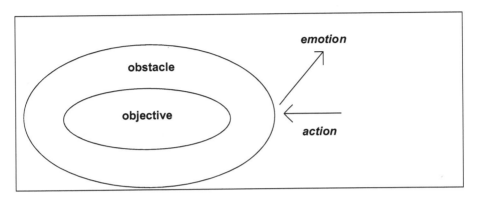

Fig. 2. An action hits an obstacle.

As you look at the diagram realize that the arrow labeled **action** is thrusting *toward* the obstacle and the arrow labeled **emotion** is darting *out from* it; emotion therefore is about *playing an action,* about *doing* something. The principle is the same as metal striking against metal; over time after constant pounding the metal will grow hot and eventually sparks will begin to fly. These 'sparks' in human beings are exertion and frustration. The supposition is that both actors are playing high-energy active verbs with all the energy they've got—that is, they are fighting to overcome outrageous situations with actions that match those situations. This I submit will lead them to the 'subconscious' spoken of by Stanislavski.[4]

---

[4] Ibid. Chapter 16, "On the Threshold of the Subconscious."

Though Emotional Memory[5] can have value early in the rehearsal process as a tool for concentration and to 'kick-start' work on the generating of emotion, I have not been completely certain of the long term reliability of it in the actual playing of a scene. True, the actor employing it is seeking to remember the surrounding and feeling of an emotional event in order to *compare* it in kind with an emotional event they are to portray fictionally in a play. This can be helpful, but it then must be taken *farther* so that it does not eventually pull an actor's full attention *away* from their scene partner. Juliet thinking about a long dead pet—or some such personal 'substitution'— in order to cry when her father renounces her is, to me, going to take herself out of the scene, away from the very object she must relate to: the *actor playing Capulet*. If she remembers her first real love when kissing the actor cast as Romeo, she is, in effect, kissing *that* person and not the person *holding her in his arms at that moment.* I say Juliet must concentrate on the *object before her*— the actor playing **Romeo.** Even after the most successful application of Emotional Memory, eventually the actress playing Juliet must find in her *live* scene partner what she can love and then do what the playwright has decided she must do—fall in love with Romeo, *that* Romeo. How does this happen? By doing: by **stroking** Romeos hair, **kissing** his cheek, **caressing** his brow, **hugging** his muscled body to her own for warmth, **delving** into his eyes with her own, etc. This is what Juliet can consciously *do* as a means to produce emotion. The same applies to the scene with her angry father Capulet: the moment he enters she must fight to ***please*** her father, to ***win*** his fatherly love, to ***prove*** to him that she is an obedient daughter! She is, in effect, offering him her *love.* All of these active verbs the actor is capable of doing without regard to feeling. It is the same for Masha's tears in *Three Sisters.* With all of her might the actress must play an action against an obstacle to get an objective—she must physicalize the diagram above. In dealing with the 'weeps violently' stage direction she must translate that *result* into *action,* which will mean, among other things, to **speak** *violently,* to **gesture** *violently* and to **reach** out with *violence.* When faced with the playing of

---

[5] Ibid. Chapter 9, "Emotion Memory."

emotion do not think of emotion as a *condition that comes over you:* think of it as a series of *actions you must perform* with all of your energy and might *because of* that emotion.

We human beings cannot help ourselves; we always experience a primal reaction as a *result* of the things we do. After all, how do you think we feel when, after offering love with all of our heart, we are *refused love in return?*


# *Picnic*

To explore the active verb and the outrageous let us examine a short scene between Howard and Rosemary in William Inge's fine award-winning play *Picnic.*

It is Act 3, Scene 1, in the wee hours of the morning after a great Labor Day celebration in a small Kansas town. Howard is returning Rosemary to her boarding house and beneath a tree in the front yard they have an uneasy, contentious conversation about the future of their relationship. Until tonight they have had a pleasant enough understanding, but it has not been altogether satisfying for Rosemary. Earlier in the play with the neighbor women she speaks of Howard disparagingly as compared to the virile Hal Carter, refusing to call Howard her, "boyfriend." But later, before the big local celebration, on a drunken impulse she pathetically throws herself at the much younger Hal only to be rebuffed, and this causes her to demand that she and Howard run off that night to escape the ugly events of the evening for some impulsive, illusive happiness outside of town. The implication is that they have just had sexual intercourse for the first time—Howard says, "You were awful nice to me tonight, Rosemary," to which Rosemary can only grumble. She is a middle-aged school teacher out of options for a lasting relationship with a man, and the events of this night have caused her to be morose and depressed. Because of what they have just done she insists that they get married: "You can't go off without me. Not after tonight. *That's* sense." They argue, intermittently worried lest those in the houses nearby might be wakened, until finally Howard gets up the gumption to speak his mind:

> HOWARD. *(After a moment's troubled thought crosses to D.L. of steps)* No. I'm not gonna marry anyone that says, "You gotta marry me, Howard." I'm not gonna. *(He is silent. Rosemary stares at him. Slowly Howard reconsiders.)* If a woman wants me to marry her...she could at least say "please."
>
> ROSEMARY. *(Beaten and humble.)* Please marry me, Howard.
>
> HOWARD. Well...you got to give me time to think it over.
>
> ROSEMARY. Oh, God! Please marry me, Howard. Please... *(Sinks to her knees.)* Please...please...
>
> HOWARD. *(Turns.)* Rosemary, don't! *(He goes to her, lifts her up.)* Honey, you go get some sleep. I'll call you in the morning.
>
> ROSEMARY. I won't sleep a wink, Howard, till I hear. *(He lifts her gently to her feet. She crosses to steps at R.— U. on top step.)* Good night, Howard.
>
> HOWARD. I'll call you first thing. *(Crosses to her— squeezes her hand.)*
>
> ROSEMARY. Good night.
>
> HOWARD. 'Night, Rosemary. *(Crosses U.C. lawn.)*
>
> ROSEMARY. *(Holding in her tears.)* Please call.
>
> HOWARD. *(Stops.)* I will, Rosemary. I will. *(Starts.)*
>
> ROSEMARY. Please call.
>
> HOWARD. *(Stops.)* Honey, don't worry.
>
> ROSEMARY. Good night.

HOWARD. Good night.    *(Picnic, Act 3, Sc 1)*

Inge has provided the outrageous for us. Rosemary, up to this moment, has been loud-mouthed, bragging, and bossy. In this scene she is up against the wall of life and she knows it. Therefore she has no choice, she is forced to lower herself to her knees and *beg* this befuddled local shop owner to marry her. This would have certainly been shocking in 1953 when the play opened on Broadway; how about now in the new millennium? How might this moment be handled by the strong, self-reliant, 'I don't need a man to be happy' woman of today? I say it would be just as shocking—if not more so. I have had female students question if they really had to perform this act when the moment came in the scene, as if it were some unseemly chore in a porno movie. What is actually unseemly—what is *outrageous*—is Rosemary feeling that she has no *alternative* but to get down on her knees, and in doing so it is this which provides pathos; we feel for this woman who was so strong when we first met her, reduced to such degradation. We are embarrassed for her when she debases herself getting down on her knees to beg.

How might we, do you think, make it even *more* outrageous? Here are some possibilities:

1. She stoops further and kisses his shoes.
2. She takes the tactic of wooing him as before and begins trying to unbutton his fly.
3. She begins to pound at him with her fists in a rage.
4. She begins to undress, casting her clothing onto the ground below. (This last one is seeking the most outrageous choice possible; I assure you I am not in the habit of asking my students to undress in a scene!)

Each of the above actions can be assigned an active verb. 1. To kiss. 2. To ravish. 3. To pummel. 4. To seduce. Additional choices can be to bow down, crawl, plead, cow (as in cow tow), wail, among others. In fact the choices in the mind of a person caught up in an outrageous situation are endless.

But what of Howard? Howard Bevins in *Picnic* is a gem of a role an actor may encounter, but it contains a trap. He is befuddled, middle-aged, absent-minded and brow-beaten. Even in the hands of a master character actor—which is as this role is usually cast— Howard will still have moments, in this scene in particular, when the actor portraying him just might have the urge to choose "To be left alone," as an objective. A horrible choice, unless Inge has penciled in at the bottom of the page, *Exits.*

You can certainly guess the outrageous situation in which Howard has been put. His girlfriend has presented him with an ultimatum; she has demanded that he marry her. He too in his way has just as few options for the future as Rosemary, but he is a male in this provincial society, he is probably at his core less ambitious than she and he just might like things as they are. But she has forced him up against the wall, after midnight in a small town where everybody knows everybody else's business, where people are apt to talk and overhear private conversations that might get overheated (add another outrageous choice for Rosemary: she screams her lines to the night sky!). For the set-in-his-ways Howard, this might well be an outrageous situation.

How about these as potential actions to further jazz him up:

1. He takes Rosemary up on her offer and begins to make love to her right there.
2. He falls to his knees and begins to weep.
3. He throws caution to the wind and begins shouting aloud at her.
4. He runs away (we know he will need to return; this can be only a tactic).

In this scene active verbs for Howard might be to calm (Rosemary), sooth, berate, attack, placate, quiet, massage, belittle, ridicule, beg, support, etc.

In both cases above it matters, *exactly,* which verb you choose. *Massage,* for instance, might be more interesting than *placate; cringe* might be more active even than *beg, stab* more active than *demand, woo* more so than *reason.* In rehearsal try as many of them as you can think of until you find a better word and a better word and then a better. This is how the big bold outrageous choice will begin to happen.

## P.S.—How You State Your *Objective* Matters, Too!

Just as crucial as making specific, exciting choices for your active verb, it is also vital that you are as equally clear on what your Objective is in the scene. As we have said, your objective is what you want to *get* as a *result* of what you *do.* When you score this on paper and convert it to your subconscious in the form of Given Circumstances, you will need to be very clear there as well. (Simply take these italicized words from the previous sentence and realize what is left: ***Get, Result, Do.*** Cool how that works, isn't it?) You are seeking to avoid the pitfall I speak about in Part Two when I state that muddy choices make for muddy acting. Therefore your Objective statement must be in the form of a simple, declarative sentence, a short, clear statement. To give you an example of what to do and what to avoid, let us return to our friend Joe who wants that $20 from Bob:

Joe's OBJECTIVE is to get Bob to loan him $20. It may also be stated in the form "I must..." This helps to create even greater need. In his score the actor playing Joe might record:

### *I MUST GET BOB TO LOAN ME $20.*

You might also say, **I MUST GET $20 FROM BOB,** or **I MUST GET $20** as you enter the scene. The point is that it is abundantly clear from the get-go what you *want.*

Sometimes student actors in their zeal to cover all bases go too far in this statement. They try to include *all* of the given circumstances of the play, all of the earlier scenes and events that affect their character. This leads to an Objective statement that might read something like this:

*I WANT BOB TO LOAN ME $20 SO THAT I CAN FIX MY CAR TIRE SO THAT I CAN GO PICK UP MY GIRLFRIEND FROM THE HOSPITAL TO SAVE HER FROM HER DOMINEERING MOTHER SO THAT SHE AND I CAN GET MARRIED SO THAT WE CAN LIVE HAPPILY EVER AFTER ETC ETC ETC BLAH BLAH BLAH....*

In this writing of the Objective—which is only meant to be about the individual scene, remember—it becomes in effect the *Super* Objective. It is the Super Objective which is meant to be broad and encompass the character's life of the entire play. The Objective is meant only for the scene *in the moment* during the act; the scenes that happen later can be fought for one by one as they come. This *present* scene is all that you have at hand and is all that is in your control or province. Therefore the Objective must be simple and specific to the *moment at hand*. Once Joe gets the $20 he can THEN go about the task of fighting for other desires. But if in the moment his present needs are muddied by all manner of other concerns his work in the scene will be rendered unclear and muddy as well. Got it, gang?

## Beats: that is, You Must *Change*

Like a diligent, hard-working acting student, you have labored tirelessly to come up with an active verb that is truly active and compels you to *do* with force and power; you are ready to go on that stage and fight for your objective and give it all you have got! And you do! You start the scene with such outrageous energy and determination that you pound your scene partner to dust! They cannot get a word in edge-wise; you are so powerful and you want them to give you what you want so desperately they certainly must fear for their life. You pound and pound and pound and...

The scene falls *flat*.

It falls flat because it is played on only one level, because you fought so hard to get what you wanted that you never *listened* to a word they said or took in the *meaning* of what they said. You ignored their tone, their need, what *they* were fighting for in the scene, as well. Bless you, you did what I asked and played your part struggling to overcome an outrageous situation caused by love. But in your enthusiasm you forgot that the scene is between *two people!* It must happen between the two of you and in order for it to build each of you must genuinely *listen* to each other and you must *register* what each other is saying—what is being "given to you"—and dear actor you must change accordingly.

Your Objective in the scene must be absolute and rock-hard until your scene partner *replies*. This is when the scene truly begins, when both characters are fighting for something and both are forced up against a wall of life, battling, giving and taking. The two of you can agree on what the stage setting looks like, what the given circumstances as set down by the playwright are, what the relationship between the two of you is, but what each of you want from the other can only be revealed in the midst of playing the scene *together*. Once in the scene you and your partner receive and react—and change *tactics*—to save your life. Then we have a play! This is why acting has also been defined as *"reacting."*

Thoughts to consider:

1. You must honestly *listen*. Really. You do not *act* listening.

2. You must fight for what you want as hard as you can until your partner forces you to take a *beat;* that is, to *change course* using an even more suggestive active verb. We do this every day of our lives when we desperately want something from someone and are not getting it; we just call it *"trying harder!"*

3. When you 'change beats' it may help to choose opposites; if you wooed them to begin with then you might attack or

accuse them now. Out of frustration we humans do this all the time, as well.

4.   When actually playing the scene, unless your new tactic demands a lower vocal level, you must maintain the vocal energy level that has been established on stage. Normally this will take care of itself as long as you are honestly listening and reacting to your partner; in a shouting argument with someone you are most likely going to shout back at them, even try to top them with your shouting. We return in kind what we think we are getting from the other person, be it good or bad. We defend ourselves if we think that we are being slighted. We "react" to what they are doing to us.

      But there is a technical reason for being aware of the vocal level of a scene. You do not want to cause the scene to suddenly drop in energy because you have spoken *softly* in reply to a shout in your face; I have seen a lot of young actors do this in working on a scene. Doing this causes the energy of the scene to drop. A dynamic in a scene must work this way: shouting stops when it *must* stop, when it has hit the ceiling and can soar no higher (your director will be very aware of this and will help you with it and in fact the playwright has probably written in the moment when the shouting must scale down). This is why if you should suddenly decide to reply softly as a *tactic* in the midst of an argument, it must indeed be thought a *better tactic, sending a stronger message* than the one you were playing before!

5.   Check the script for when, in the midst of your partners' lines, you are moved to speak. I am not speaking about your normal 'cue' line here; that is when the playwright has made your scene partner stop talking. I am speaking about the moment your partner speaks a single *word* which demands your response at once! Most of the time this will occur well before your partner has even finished talking. Take the cue line from Howard in our scene from *Picnic.*

When Howard finally speaks and says, 'No,' for the first time, Rosemary should be leaping to reply *the moment she heard it*, even though Howard has not finished. "No" is actually Rosemary's 'cue' because it is this word which *she least wanted to hear* and it is this word that drives her to answer back! For the actress playing Rosemary it might even happen—which is always a welcome accident—that she winds up over-lapping Howard, interrupting his last words. This will not harm the scene; it will only make it more immediate. You can always apologize afterward to your scene partner for cutting them off (I speak about these ideas later; you must act *on* the line and you must *earn* a pause). We do this all the time in real life, right?

## EXERCISE:
## THE MOMENT BEFORE

Here is an exercise to help scene partners energize and jump-start their scene. It is a very handy warm up to get you 'into' your scene. It begins like this:

- Play an improvisation based on *all* of the scenes that happen to your character *before* the present scene begins. In other words, if the scene you are working on is in Act 2, Scene 3, take *all* the events of Act I and Act 2 Scene 1 and 2 and combine them, performing them in *your own words.*

- Take these prior given circumstances—the *gist*—of what happened before your scene began and make up an active, contentious fight between the two of you. Kick and attack and soothe and woo your partner with all the energy you've got.

- After allowing the improv to play for a few moments, the acting teacher/monitor will shout, "Stop!" and the two of you will immediately begin your real scene in Act 2, Scene 3.

• You will now play the scene as rehearsed, with the actual lines.

What should happen is that you will still be breathing hard from the histrionics you have just improvised; the scene should be newly energized and driven by what has *gone on before,* and what's more it can build even higher by having been fueled with what is in the *present* scene! The value of this exercise is that it is not only text based but also it helps the actor start the scene with heightened energy and need; there is no lag time at the beginning due to the actors trying to "warm up" or "get into it." Starting at such a high level also makes it more possible that the actors will discover impulses and choices that will be more outrageous or at the least choices with greater stakes. This is similar to an acting class tool I learned from famed stage actor Morris Carnovsky[6] many years ago, when he would get actors to jump start their scene by using a shouting argument speaking only the words 'Yes!' and 'No!' When you allow it to play for a few moments, to run its normal course of humans squabbling with one another, a lot of fun exciting things can be created that had never happened before. This Moment Before exercise is even better because their impulses are connected directly to what actually happens in the play.

EXERCISE:
ONE WORD BEAT CHANGE

This exercise gives actors the challenge of playing a scene from beginning to end with only one word each as their 'dialogue.'

---

[6] Morris Carnovsky (1897—1992) was an American stage and film actor and founding member of the Group Theatre (1931-37). He is best known for his sympathetic portrayal of Shylock in *The Merchant of Venice* and as the title role in *King Lear,* both with the American Shakespeare Theatre in Stratford, Conn. In later years he was renowned as an acting teacher.

It is similar to its variation, Yes/No, but I added this difference; the actors play the full, script-based *subtext* of their scene but can only reply with **one word** in answer to the other actor. Both actors are playing objectives, using actions to get what they want, but can only do so with a *single word* that distills everything they wish to say in that lone response.

Let us look again at *Picnic,* returning to the scene with Howard and Rosemary: Howard says No he will not marry her and she is forced to shamelessly drop to her knees and beg him to change his mind. Suppose the scene—the very same scene—has as dialogue not what Inge wrote but rather the *sense and essence* of what those characters want from each other in the scene, reduced to a *single word?*

Possible choices are listed below, along with the possible *subtext* underneath each one-word line:

|  | Says: | Which Means: |
|---|---|---|
| HOWARD. | Can't. | I won't do it |
| ROSEMARY. | Shock. | We had sex tonight! |
| HOWARD. | Bullied. | Stop pressuring me! |
| ROSEMARY. | Changed. | Sex changes things! |
| HOWARD. | Ask. | Don't tell me what to do! |
| ROSEMARY. | Lost. | I'm desperate!<br>(Drops to her knees) |
| HOWARD. | Sympathy. | You're degrading yourself! |
| ROSEMARY. | Hopeless. | I don't give a damn! |

The single words are about what you *really want* from your scene partner and what you are willing to do, *must* do, to make them give it to you. It is also an excellent gauge of just how clear the actor is on their objective. I have seen actors, who had already memorized their actual lines in the scene and even worked on the scene in class, suddenly get tongue-tied and confused at the prospect of coming up with only *one word* to respond to their partner! Why? Because they are not completely clear on *what they want from the other actor*. This lack of clarity will instead make them fall back on the scene and attempt, in effect, to play the *actual* scene lines though they are only saying one word; they will begin to halt and pause, stumbling in their mind as they try to see the script in their head, struggling to pick a single word out of their lines to represent what they want in the improv. This is not what the improvisation is about! It is about the actor *listening* to the other actor and responding with *need*, in fact *more* need because they cannot respond until they have been given the *inciting* word from their partner. In this regard the scene is also about the Illusion of the First Time,[7] playing Objectives and Beats, Talking and Listening. The actor is forced to use their imagination in the moment as they fight against the obstacle of *I must listen to my partner and I can only reply with one word.* This makes the actors need each other even more in the scene.

---

[7] William Gillette (1853-1937) *The Illusion of the First Time in Acting,* (Dramatic Museum of Columbia University, 1915) 39.

# 5. The Magic If, "2.0"

All these you may avoid but the Lie Direct; and you may avoid that, too, with an 'if.' I knew when seven justices could not take up a quarrel, but when the parties were met themselves, one of them thought but of an 'if', as 'if you said so, then I said so', and they shook hands and swore brothers. Your 'if' is the only peacemaker; much virtue in 'if.'

*As You Like It*

Lord, we know what we are, but know not
What we may be.

*Hamlet*

Stanislavski's Magic If remains a cornerstone in the work of the actor. In *The Stanislavski System, Elements of an Action,* Sonia Moore writes (italics are hers):

> *If* carries the actor into the imaginary circumstances. In asking, "What would I do *if* I were..."an actor does not have to force himself to believe that he is such a person in such circumstances. *If* is a supposition, and it does not imply or assert anything that exists. [8]

I have a new way I should like for you to think of the Magic If. I call it The Magic If **2.0** and I state it like this: *How do I do what*

---

[8] Sonia Moore, *The Stanislavski System, Elements of an Action,* Penguin Books, 1984.

*the playwright has decided I MUST do?* This has come out of years of acting students decrying, "But I wouldn't do that if I was that person in those circumstances!" Simplest put, at its best the Magic If is, ultimately, always about *doing* something. It is what Stanislavski called the "conscious to the subconscious."[9] The search for genuine human feeling by the actor is best done *indirectly* through the conscious and consistent playing of physical actions. It is as if you are seeking to move a brick wall with your bare hands and you finally collapse in a sodden heap after the tenth time you failed.

The Magic If, it can be said, is giving an adult name to the child's game of make-believe. To ask an actor 'what would you do if you were that person in those circumstances?' (with the implication being that you are hoping they will then see themselves doing what the character in the *script* does ) can be *beside the point*. Think of small children playing on the beach, building sand castles and war fortresses, adding little plastic soldiers to storm imaginary enemy forces. Have you ever heard a child say, "I can't play this game. What's my *motivation"?* No. What do children do? Depending upon the game they will *jump right in*, with the decision of who is the good guy and who is the bad guy already understood (accepting that next time the roles will switch) and they *play!* They do not require the assurance of motivation, reality or feeling that grown up actors require.

With The Magic If 2.0 I am suggesting this:

- The Given Circumstances alone are motivation for the actor.
- The obligation to DO is the most important thing.
- The actor must do what the playwright has written they do even if they do not understand why.
- The actor accepts that their own personal confusion is not unlike the possible confusion in their character.
- Doing does not rely upon emotion or feeling.

---

[9] Ibid. Chapter 16,"On the Threshold of the Subconscious."

- Emotional discovery is possible for the actor as a result of this doing.
- Doing is professional because it can be consciously repeated.

Let me illustrate with this conversation between myself and a young actor playing Othello:

OTHELLO. I know I believe that my wife has been cheating on me, but how do I play killing Desdemona at the end? I wouldn't do that if I was Othello in those circumstances. I admit that I'd be mad as hell, but enough to actually kill her? I don't think I could be that mad. And besides, I've never killed anybody; how can I possibly know what it's like?

HERB P. William Shakespeare has decided that Othello must kill Desdemona in the final scene, out of a need to restore and preserve his honor. As motivation—or confusion, if you want to think of it that way—you can begin by using what I think is clear uncertainty in the text when Othello kisses his sleeping wife, saying, *"O balmy breath that dost almost persuade / Justice to break her sword! One more, one more. / Be thus when thou art dead, and I will kill thee, / and love thee after!"* Also, I suggest that you concentrate not on what *you* would do if you were Othello in that situation, but rather *how do you do what the playwright has decided you must do?*

OTH. How do I—do what the *playwright* has decided I must do?

HP. Yes. Remember even in the script Othello *does not want* to kill his wife, he *must* kill her. 'Yet she must die, else she'll betray more men,' he says. Your performance in the role will only be enriched by the very human uncertainty and confusion that comes out of the knowledge that you do not want to do something but you must do it. In this regard you truly need never have experienced anything of this sort because the character you are playing in the moment has never experienced it before, *either. Othello himself* has never done it. Shakespeare has even helped you with the number of lines that are spoken. I direct you back to the script; Othello speaks 22 lines of iambic pentameter before Desdemona even wakes; after that 66 more lines are spoken before she is dead. If Othello was so hell bent on killing his wife why did he not just do it as soon as he came into her chamber? Why speak the long "It is the cause" speech, and after she wakes why bother with saying he will allow her to pray before her death? Why accuse her of giving the handkerchief to Cassio? In the text alone does not this suggest at least *some* hesitation, some trepidation on his part? Therefore you need not struggle to *motivate* what you do; you only need to accept that it must be *done.*

OTH. But shouldn't everything we do be motivated?

HP. Absolutely, and Othello – you—already have the motivation; Iago has convinced you that she has made you a cuckold by having an affair with Cassio, she has dishonored you by doing this and to regain your honor you must take her life. Within that there is still room for fragile, fallible human beings to have *doubts,* and that is the scene played out before finally she is strangled. We are constantly doing things we cannot explain, for which it is impossible to show the motivation for. There are rich, compelling acting values that can be found when the actor is available to the uncertainty of not knowing *why, or how or what for.* As long as you do *something*—even if you fear that it may be wrong—you will still be serving the play, the scene and your work, with results that have never been thought of before because they were *allowed to happen out of never having been planned.* To me, this is the best iteration of William Gillette's "Illusion of the First Time."

OTH. Then I must only concentrate on what the character *does* in that situation?

HP. Yes.

OTH. And will this make what the character does in that situation real and believable for me?

HP. Yes; believable because you *do* it. But even the *unreality* of it all will help you; people always do things they themselves cannot understand, yet they go ahead and do them anyway. After behaving badly about something have you ever in your life said to yourself, 'That wasn't like me; what made me act like that?' Do not fear the confusion or uncertainty of doing something you normally would not do; this will merely cause you to act like every other human being that has ever lived! I cannot say this enough; *just do it*, even in the most outrageous of situations, and you will be helped by the realization that perhaps the character *does not want to do it either* and finds it just as outrageous as you do! Othello does not want to kill Desdemona. He *must* do it!

OTH. And this will make it real for me every time?

HP. Don't get hung up on 'making it real' for yourself. That is a question which is rendered moot because you have put on the costume and agreed to perform the role. The fact that it is not *real* is immaterial; in fact the *feelings* of the actor are immaterial as far as the performance is concerned! Theatre after all is illusion. Either real or unreal playing an action will serve you because it can be performed over and over again without regard for the reality of the individual; it is an action fully in control of the person performing it.

OTH. But how can the doing help me *feel* something?

HP. Once again, you need not concern yourself with feeling. You must devote yourself to *doing*. Unless the play is a one-person show (and probably even then!), it is not in a vacuum. There are consequences to doing what you do; you will be confronted at once by the other characters that will wish to know why you did what you did and attempt to prevent you from doing it! They will challenge you and you will have to fight for yourself with the only reasons the playwright has given you, which may not be enough to you, may not be contained in your ken of knowledge, but even they must be offered with all of your might because you are now being challenged by the very townspeople of Venice. The fight you have with the Venetians at the end of the play is real enough because they are fighting you and you must defend yourself; that will provide you with sufficient feeling to start. As far as grief over killing Desdemona is concerned you should not have to force that. You did not want to kill her in the first place! When the moment comes concentrate on the *doing,* on the active verb, on making that as much of a reaction to an outrageous situation as you can possibly make it—and it is an outrageous situation because you have just killed the woman you truly love!—and you will not need to force emotion. At the end of the play, in your final speech, perhaps you might even play the action of *'To Apologize'* (to Desdemona's corpse)?

OTH. Isn't it important that I feel something?

HP. In the actual doing and performing of your action, NO. Emotion is a *bi-product* of you fighting to defend yourself. This is true if you are Amanda Wingfield or King Lear. Feeling comes from the *doing;* often it will come *even as* you are playing the action. But even then, still, the actor must not consciously seek that feeling because feelings are unreliable; concentrate on the doing until the objective is won, even if the objective is interrupted by events in the play. Even and especially then!

OTH. One last question: why not just *pretend* that I am feeling it? Why not simply try to *show* the audiences that I am feeling it, by collapsing, trying to cry, like that?

HP. Because your honest, human reaction is far more interesting and powerful and *unique* than any that is erroneously forced out of you. Don't ask me how but I guess there are some actors who can produce tears at the drop of a hat; good for them. I am not altogether certain that such ability is related to the text at hand, but just the same kudos to them. But *genuine* emotion, that which can be believed whether there is the *presence of tears or not,* works more reliably for an actor when it comes as the result of playing an action against an obstacle. This is within the province of the actor; doing rather than feeling. Othello may not be consciously seeking emotion in the scene, but he can *proclaim* to the stars that Desdemona has betrayed him, he can *accuse* her of giving Cassio the handkerchief and he can *punish* her for weeping over Cassio's death to his face! All of these are actions you as Othello can play, these are things you can *do*. When you end her life it is by *smothering* with a pillow and then you *press harder* because she is not yet dead and you do *not want her to suffer*—that is, you can show her mercy! All of these acts are in your control, they do not rely on emotion to perform them, and all that is required is *physical energy*. Even in the performing of an action we cannot help ourselves; we feel something about what we have done, both before and after we have done it. This is how you approach the playing of emotion.

# 6. What if Nothing is Happening in the Scene?

Smooth runs the water where the brook is deep.

*2 Henry VI*

Sometimes in the most moving of plays there is a scene that manages to escape the actor's imagination because it just seems nothing is going on. This often occurs in Modern drama, in the realistic plays of Ibsen and Chekhov and the naturalism of Strindberg, but it can also be found in plays of today, as well. Many contemporary works seem to be written with almost the intention of being eventually adapted to film (such as the work of Neil LaBute and David Mamet, who by the way have also become prominent film directors as well as successful screenwriters); they are characterized by quick black-out scenes, short-sentenced dialogue and almost nothing in the way of stage directions. My theory is that these playwrights, in addition to whatever else they may be trying to do, are seeking more subtlety as they infuse their words with *subtext,* relying as much as possible upon the words alone as a guide for the performer. In their skillful hands scenes of enormous power are created without any question of something "going on" in the midst of them.

But there are those plays and scenes that can still be difficult for the actor to decipher. Presented here are a few scenes, both from

45

the past and the present, in which it might be tricky finding the action because one of the characters appear either to be holding back or doing very little to fight for an objective:

## ROCKET TO THE MOON by Clifford Odets

### Ben Stark and Cleo Singer

### Act Two Sc. 1

I like introducing the plays of Odets to young actors. Odets, because of his near poetic, fast-talking, 1930's-style dialogue forces the actor of today to work harder on subtext because the words of his people ring so differently to our ear; at face value the dialogue can seem phony and corny. Actually I find Odets' dialogue almost Shakespearean in that it sounds *heightened;* all his characters in their own way are good talkers, they enjoy a certain turn of phrase, but most of all I believe they speak with a *need* borne out of being the denizens of a vast teeming metropolis in the throes of an economic depression, they have been made aware of the uncertainty of life because of one World War and are wary of facing the threat of another.

This scene has the pitfall of one character seeming to hold back. Even if that is what actually is going on the scene can still be made much more active for both actors.

Ben Stark is a middle-aged dentist whose marriage and practice have fallen upon hard times. He has hired Cleo Singer as secretary. She is a vibrant, hopeful, needy New York waif with false dreams of becoming a dancer. Eventually they fall into a torrid love affair.

This scene is before that happens, but if you study it carefully you can see the real needs of both people that make the affair inevitable.

I speak to the actors:

HP. (To Stark) What do you want from Cleo?

STARK. I want *her*—I guess.

HP. Why do you 'guess?'

S. Because I—seem to hold back.

HP. Keep that thought. You seem to hold back. (To Cleo) What do you want from him?

CLEO. His—understanding?

HP. How about his love?

C. Yes; his love. But—

HP. But what?

C. He seems—kind of distant.

HP. Remember I don't allow the phrase 'kind of.'

C. He seems distant.

HP. Why?

S. It's not that; I just—can't—I have a wife.

HP. But your marriage is on the rocks, right?

S. Right.

HP. And earlier in the scene she says that you can be evasive, that you hold back. Is that true?

S. Yes.

HP. So why do you stay in the scene?

S. Because Odets hasn't written that I 'exit.'

HP. Smart aleck. But correct; that means…

S. That I *must* stay.

HP. Right. And—

S. That I *have* to talk to her.

HP. Correct. Let's get back to the given circumstances. Your marriage is on the rocks, your practice is failing, you are strapped for cash, you are middle aged and you can be 'evasive.'

S. Yes.

HP. Why do you stay here to listen to Cleo?

S. She's—really alive.

HP. Alive?

S. Energetic.

HP. She's a terrible secretary, don't you allude to that?

S. Yes; but—I don't really mind.

HP. Good. Why?

S. Because she's—

HP. Yes, because she's alive. What makes her alive?

S. She has dreams, of being a dancer, of escaping her small apartment where she is cramped with her relatives, where her father died—

HP. She wants to escape a hard life. Is that it?

S. Yes.

HP. (to Cleo) Is that it?

C. Yes; I have it hard at home.

HP. This is the scene—although it probably begins to happen earlier—when you are exposed as having lied about being a rich kid who doesn't have to work. Actually you're a poor working girl who desperately needs this job, in more ways than one. Right?

C. Yes.

HP. Stark questions you about a big Broadway producer, who happens to be one of his patients, because you have claimed earlier to know him.

C. Yes. He has—found me out.

HP. (To Stark) You have found her out. But you don't really challenge her very much, do you? You are careful in exposing her. Why don't you fire her? She offers to quit.

S. I—don't want to?

HP. I agree. Why?

S. Because—she—she *interests* me?

HP. Her energy? Her life?

S. Her hopes, dreams.

HP. Why would hopes and dreams 'interest' you?

S. Because I—don't have them myself?

HP. Very good. So you choose to sit and listen to her talk.

S. Yes.

HP. Is that all you do?

S. Well…

HP. How about a different word than *interest*. A more outrageous word.

S. Well. Moves me?

HP. Not bad. Get the Thesaurus out. How about *enthralls* you? *Draws* you? Pulls you? Captivates you? *Intoxicates* you?

S. Attracts?

HP. Good. So what do you want from her?

S. I want her—love?

HP. Good choice; always the best choice. But you don't seem to do anything about it. In this scene.

C. I tell him that he holds back; he just occasionally smiles.

HP. Why does he 'hold back' again?

C. Because of his wife.

HP. Maybe. But his wife is not here. Only you are. And he is. He stays in the room to listen to you because you captivate him. Stark: suppose you do not yet know that you love her? What could you want in this scene then? Just this scene?

S. Well...

HP. You say that she attracts you. We just ran through those other possibilities.

S. I stay because she makes me feel good.

HP. Excellent! Therefore you want—?

S. I want her to make me feel good by talking about *herself?*

HP. Great. Because you get out of that—what?

S. Good feeling?

HP. How about escape?

S. Escape?

HP. Yes, *escape*. Escape from your failing marriage and nagging wife and broken practice during the depression. *Escape to the hope of a better life.* Is that possible?

S. Yes.

HP. That makes you just like her; both of you want to escape to the hope of a better life. Maybe even Cleo knows in her heart that she has no hope but she is at least willing to *dream* of that hope. Is that possible, Cleo?

C. Yes; very.

HP. Is it worth it?

C. Yes.

HP. Is it worth it to you, Stark?

S. Yes.

HP. Is all this worth fighting for? This—*dream of hope?*

S. Yes.

HP. Worth throwing your wife over for?

S. Yes—well—

HP. At least *thinking about* throwing your wife over for?

S. Yes.

HP. And maybe—later—you *then* fall in love with her? In other words, you don't know at the top of this scene that you want her.

S. Yes.

HP. Because not knowing gives you *somewhere to go* if you discover it later, right?

S. Yes, right.

HP. So what do you want from her in this scene?

S. I—want her to make me feel better?

HP. Does *cheer you up* get at it?

S. Yes; that's good. She cheers me up.

HP. Because—?

S. Because I feel better when she talks about—

HP. *Dreams* about—

S. Dreams about her life, her future, in my presence?

HP. Sounds good. Why?

S. Because I don't have dreams of my own? I don't *yet* have the guts to dream them for myself?

HP. Good. Is that why you keep her on? Even though she is a lousy secretary?

S. Yes. I guess so. *Yes.*

HP. And she is, after all, not bad on the eyes, is she?

S. Yes!

HP. So what do you do in this scene? *Actively?*

S. I listen—

HP. Not good enough.

S. An active verb?

HP. What do you do when you discover that you desperately want to hear what someone is saying?

S. I—lean forward?

HP. That's a start. Lean forward. How about clamor? As in, *toward*? Imagine a soldier in a foxhole crawling on his belly to a safer spot among his comrades. *Clamor.* Or *crawl.* How about dig? Don't worry; I'm not suggesting that you get down on all fours and beg like a dog. These are simply active verbs meant to incite you to *do*. How about devour? As in 'her every word?' Or maybe *hang*, as 'upon her lips?' You do all of these things—and you can do them regardless of what your line says, what your actual line is—because what you want is to be with her so that she can make you feel good by confessing to you her dreams and in doing this you discover that you are in love with her!

S. That'll work.

HP. There's something else that you consciously actively do in the scene.

S. What?

HP. You *smile* at her.

C. Yes; he does!

HP. It may be the only truly active thing Odets has written for you in the scene. Cleo calls you on it. She mentions it *four* times! Why do you think you do this?

S. It's—my way of showing her that I *like* her?

HP. Sounds good to me. Of course it could also be a tactic to avoid doing anything *else*. (To Cleo) What do you want from him?

C. I want to escape, too!

HP. Excellent. From what?

C. My boring, dead-end hard life, cramped in a small apartment with my family where my father died and my sister prostitutes herself.

HP. Great. And you do this—you get this escape by…?

C. Dreaming in front of his eyes?

HP. Good. 'To dream' is good. Other active verbs?

C. Confess?

HP. Yes. Also declare, admit, own up to, spill—as in *guts.*

C. How about *rhapsodize?*

HP. Fantastic. Remember you are dreaming out loud. It doesn't need to be real or possible; it doesn't have to be what you can actually attain. It is a *dream.* You got it. So—what is happening in this scene?

C. & S. A lot.

HP. And you want—you need—?

C. & S. *Each other.*

HP. Bingo.


## THE CHILDREN'S HOUR by Lillian Hellman

### Karen and Cardin

### Act 3

Lillian Hellman's ground-breaking play *The Children's Hour* was probably shocking when it first appeared on Broadway in 1934 but in the new millennium the question of homosexuality and lesbianism hardly even brings a raised eyebrow. Therefore this pivotal scene in Act 3 can be a challenge. Karen, a school teacher and founder of a private boarding school for girls, has been accused of being in a lesbian relationship with her co-founder Martha. Karen has been engaged to Joseph Cardin, but the relationship has gone sour after a long, protracted libel trial which Karen and Martha lost, costing them both their jobs and reputation.

In this scene Cardin has come to the school for the last time to break off the engagement so that the scandal which has tainted the two women will no longer damage his medical practice. It is not long, in the scene, before Karen realizes that her husband-to-be no longer supports her and in fact is searching for the first opportunity to be set free.

Hellman was influenced by the work of Ibsen and her plays are often characterized as "Well Made," which means that the overall structure is stream-lined, nothing is wasted, the action is cause and affect A to B realism. Because of this it can sometimes appear that very little goes on in scenes where it is so very important to lay groundwork of exposition for the resolution at the plays' end.

I talk to the two actors in the scene.

HP. What is happening in the scene?

CARDIN. It looks like I am trying to dump my girlfriend.

KAREN. He's dumping me.

HP. Good. Cardin you just said, '*looks* like.' What's the problem?

C. I don't come right out and say it. I keep hemming and hawing, stalling.

K. He keeps beating around the bush. The scene is slow and too careful, too 'above board.'

HP. Why does he do this, do you think? This 'hemming and hawing?' This 'stalling?'

C. Because it was the 1930's? They couldn't come right out and say it like we would today?

K. Can it be he's not certain?

HP. So he should just come in and say, 'bye-bye, baby?'

C. Well, no…

HP. Why doesn't he just do that?

K. Well. Like you say, if Hellman had wanted that she would have written *exits* at the bottom of the page.

HP. Good. So he must stay. At least until he has said his piece, right? There would be no scene between them if he just left, even though he may want to leave right away. What else?

C. He loves her?

HP. Good. Excellent choice. Best choice of all; always look for the love. Tell me about it.

C. He loves her, or he has, and he does not want to leave her.

HP. But?

C. But he wants to keep on being a doctor, he wants to continue his medical practice, he has to go on living in this town. He doesn't want to be guilty by association.

K. Karen and Martha have to leave because they lost their lawsuit.

HP. Does Karen love him?

K. Yes.

HP; Good. How much?

K. A lot?

HP: Good. How about a *whole* lot? But why does she tell him to go at the end of the scene?

K. Because she loves him.

HP. And?

K. And she knows half way through the scene that he does not trust her anymore, he actually believes that she and Martha are lovers.

HP. Yes. But why be noble? Why not try harder to convince him?

K. Hellman has decided she has to do this.

HP. Absolutely. Good. But can a character resist their author?

K. What?

HP. You must do this because Hellman has decided that you must do it; that's a given circumstance. But in the playing of it do you really have to *want* to do it? How about you do it even though you don't understand why—you only *think* you know why—but actually you dismiss him and even as you are doing it you are on the verge of losing it because you do not want to do it? No false bravery, or modesty or honor. A fallible, fragile human being driven to the breaking point who does something even they do not understand in the midst of an outrageous situation caused by love. Is that possible?

K. I guess. But she seems almost—angry at him, urging him to go—

HP. I suppose it could be possible that in this section we could have a little bit of the playwright talking—we will never know of course—but even so you are only obligated to do what the playwright has decided that you must do; *how you get there is up to you.* Most often it probably has been played that, in this last act, after having gone through so much, Karen heroically finds the courage to tell her fiancée to leave her because she realizes that he no longer trusts her though he might still love

her, and so releases him. That is the strong, resolute, wise—
*feminist*—thing to do when someone finally gets the will and
self respect to rise up and stand up and move forward to face an
uncertain future. Like Nora in *A Doll's House.* But suppose, in
releasing him, she breaks down, cracks up, is only too human
because she *loves this man* more than ever and, what's more,
*needs* him more than ever but life circumstance—that which has
been created by Ms. Hellman of course—has forced her to do
this horrible thing for her own good.

K. So I play it even more that she does not want to let him go?

HP. I think it can be more interesting if we see a person who is
genuinely struggling rather than one who is being heroic and
resolute. The rest of us are not sure how we would react in a
situation in which courage is demanded; maybe we might fail—
or *fear* we might fail! And this causes us to empathize with
Karen's, and Cardin's, dilemma.

C. I can see how Cardin would really be like this; he wants her
forgiveness—

HP. Forgiveness is good; her *absolution.*

C. Yes; he wants that desperately. He might not have come here
one last time at all had he not wanted to get her to let him go
with her blessing. He felt guilty.

HP. Exactly. Good way to put it. As a matter of fact a good
objective for him in the scene might be "I must win Karen's
Blessing."

C. That's good.

HP. Just don't fall into the pitfall of playing Cardin as a sniveling
coward. A blackguard.

C. Got it. He's a *good* guy forced to do a *bad* thing.

HP. Excellent. And notice how you got the antithesis in there, too!

K. What might my objective be?

HP. How about, *"I must convince him to stay?"*

K. Really? But I let him go.

HP. But you do not know that yet. Not at the beginning of the scene. As a matter of fact, even if you were suspicious that that was why he was there—to get you to let him off the hook—it makes sense to me that you would fight *that much harder* to make him stay. Even as you are telling him to leave you are desperately begging him to stay! More opposites, you notice? Then the scene can be a compelling moment between two good people doing the best they can rather than a slow, quiet, well-behaved parting. Screw well-behaved partings! This is *theatre!*

PROOF by David Auburn

Catherine and Hal

Act Two Sc. 5

Here is another scene which at first glance might appear to be one sided or in danger of one character avoiding engagement with another. It is the final scene of the play, in which Hal admits to Catherine that he has been wrong in thinking that she did not write the mathematical proof.

The pitfall is for the actress playing Catherine; it is easy to fall into playing "Leave me alone I don't want to talk to you!"

HP. (To Catherine) What do you want from Hal?

CATHERINE. I want him to leave me alone.

HP. Then why don't you just get up and leave?

C. The playwright hasn't written that I exit.

HP. Then how do you get him to leave you alone?

C. Oh. I see.

HP. You might want him to 'leave you alone.' It might work; it just depends on how you fight for it. What might you *do* to get him to leave you alone?

C. I—am rude to him?

HP. A state of being; rudeness is a state of being. What do you do to prove to him that you want him to leave you alone? What do you *do* to show him *rudeness?*

C. I—speak to him harshly…at him.

HP. How do you speak 'harshly?'

C. I—*snap* at him?

HP. Good. Go on.

C. Grumble?

HP. Good, yes, those are active verbs, yes, you can do those. Go on.

C. I attack him; I growl at him; I sneer at him…

HP. Good. You've got some actions you can play to *get him to leave you alone.* But he doesn't leave you alone, does he?

C. No.

HP. What does he do?

C. He stays; he keeps talking.

HP. About what?

C. About the proof. About how he was wrong, how he was wrong not to trust me when I said that I wrote it.

HP. Since he keeps talking, in fact tries to apologize for misjudging you, is there a chance your objective changes during the scene?

C. What?

HP. Is it possible that you change your mind during the scene and want something else from him?

C. Oh. Yes.

HP. What is that?

C. Well. I say that he should have trusted me.

HP. Good. Script-based motivation, given circumstances. What else do you say to him?

C. What else?

HP. He goes on and on and you say to him that he should have trusted you. You say something else, don't you? When you tell him to just go and pretend that he wrote the proof?

C. He—

HP. Yes?

C. I sarcastically shout at him that he got me in bed and got the notebook too!

HP. Right. Why do you say that?

C. To hurt him?

HP. Good. How about also because he hurt you too?

C. Oh. Yes.

HP. Is there a chance that you do not want him to leave you alone? *Because* he hurt you?

C. What?

HP. What do you want from him in the scene?

C. I want to—get back at him for hurting me?

HP. Possibly. And you get this by—? Active verbs, please. Start with those you mentioned earlier.

C. Attack, growl, sneer...

HP. Yes, to start. Great.

C. So on the outside, because I keep on refusing him—verb—it might seem like I want him to leave me alone, but actually because of our relationship I want to get back at him, to hurt him because he hurt me?

HP. Which is very different. The playwright has already decided that the two of you must talk. It may be that the reason for this is that there is still unfinished business between you, related not to the proof in the notebook but rather to the failure of trust in your relationship. The play, at this point, becomes about *love* rather than about mathematical theorems.

C. You keep telling us that every play is about love.

HP. And about outrageous situations, caused by love. It's possible—I am only guessing here—that the theme of the play is about how human relationships can break down and get clouded by confusing, hazy reasons—like the difficulty of solving math problems. Math might be the *metaphor* for those things that get in our way in life.

C. I am trying to get back at Hal because—I *love* him.

HP. I can't think of a better choice. Then that makes the actions you perform earlier in the scene *active messages you send him* in order to achieve that. You are far from holding back, you are moving forward actively doing something. This is the difference between a **positive** choice—which advances the play's action— and a *negative* choice, which brings the story to a screeching halt. You must always make a choice, which by its nature compels you to *need* the other person in the scene. One other thing: how about an outrageous action for the scene?

C. How about—I grab the notebook from his hands and beat him over the head with it?

HP. Excellent.


## Chekhov? *Funny?*

Among playwrights that are considered boring, in whose plays it seems that nothing ever happens, none can top the list ahead of poor, great Anton Chekhov. It seems that the mere mention of him can send actors either screaming from the theatre or choosing to wallow in the gloom and doom seriousness perceived to dominate his plays. Either way, both of these attitudes are grossly misguided.

In Chapter 3, I mentioned the wrenching scene between Toozenbach and Irina in the fourth act of Chekhov's *The Three*

*Sisters*. Critics argue over whether or not his work was comedy or drama; in my reading of his plays I enjoy them because Chekhov is able, in my view, to so seamlessly fuse together the comedic and the tragic.

To try to illustrate this and also address the notion of Chekhov's plays being about gloom and doom in which "nothing happens," let us discuss his "Scenes from Country Life" play, *Uncle Vanya*.

For me this play epitomizes the wonderful amalgam of comedy and tragedy which Chekhov perfected in his work; In Act II after the storm Vanya chases Yelena about the room, proclaiming his love and begging her to requite it; later in the same act Yelena and Sonia are at one moment weeping over their misspent lives and the next are laughing like school girls at the prospect of playing the piano. Chekhov has so masterfully constructed this scene that it is truly funny when later, upon returning after asking the old doctor if they might play, Sonia is forced to reply that Serebryakov's answer is, "No!" This ends the act (I am certain with laughter). In Act III after Yelena has asked Dr. Astrov if it is possible for him to love Sonia, Astrov then commences to chase *her* around the room, proclaiming *his* love, (which in small part in Act IV in the form of a farewell kiss Yelena returns). And the 'comedy' does not stop there; at the end of Act III Vanya chases Serebryakov about the stage, firing a pistol after him, missing every step of the way. He is finally forced to slump hopelessly into a chair, proclaiming, "Missed again!" Earlier Vanya had exploded with a moving tirade directed at the old doctor for proposing to sell the estate on which Vanya has labored all of his life. This is Chekhov's hand at work; rather than dreary and hopeless his characters are passionate and energetic; they 'protest too much' about an unhappy life, they shout and cry and sing out loud in the wake of this 'unhappiness.' This is how they can feel sadness so deeply one moment and the next moment laugh uproariously about it and it is this that makes them so human—*just like us*.

I would suggest that this is a most helpful interpretation when approaching the plays of Anton Chekhov: the plays are realistic, to be sure, but they also call for a *heightened* reality, a theatrical reality bursting past the footlights with people who feel, love and hate deeply. In Chekhov's work always look for, in addition to the love, the *passion* in the heart of his people and you will be well on your way to presenting a rich evening of theatre that is filled with the joyous human fusion of opposites which is antithesis. This is perhaps what some directors avoid doing when working on his one 'dramatic' play *The Three Sisters*. *Three Sisters* has gotten a bad rap. Yes, the ladies do not get to Moscow—but I think they never *wanted to go* to Moscow! Their loud, constant proclamations of, "To Moscow!" I see as *metaphor* for restlessness, the longing for a more exciting, interesting life; the kind their passion demanded. The tragedy is they never found what that exciting substitution was; Olga was able to do no better than teaching at the school; Irina no better than marrying the ill-fated Toozenbach and Masha winds up not with Vershinin but saddled with her bumbling schoolmaster husband Kulygin. Their desires are real, their tools to win those desires faulty. This to me is the glory of Chekhov; at best this is what his plays are capable of.

I am also a fan of Chekhov because in scenes like those of *Uncle Vanya* the playwright has introduced the outrageous for us: what can be more outrageous than chasing after a man with a gun and firing, firing and missing, *on stage?*

## Ibsen? Outrageous?

### HEDDA GABLER by Henrik Ibsen

### Hedda and Judge Brack

### Act 4

It is too obvious to select the final scene of *A Doll's House* as proof of a play's outrageous situation—What could be more outrageous in 1879 than a wife choosing to leave her husband and children?—so I have chosen the final scene of Ibsen's later play, *Hedda Gabler*. In this case the question is not so much about the lack of action—rather, it is how far and how outrageous the actors might make this circumstance set in 1891.

I talk with the actors.

HP. (To Hedda) What is happening in this scene?

HEDDA. I find out that my life is over.

HP. (To Brack) What is happening in this scene?

JUDGE BRACK. I am letting Hedda know that I own her now.

HEDDA. Which will mean that my life is over.

HP. I agree with both choices. Good. Why?

H. Because I will be in his clutches, at his beck and call, for the rest of my life. I am at the mercy of his blackmail.

HP. At his beck and call—for *what?*

H. *Sex.*

HP. Excellent. So the scene is easy, isn't it?

H. We don't know how far to go; how far to—take it.

JB. It's the 1890's. I can't even touch her, can I?

HP. Well she is a married woman, too, for that matter. Married to your *friend,* George Tesman.

H. What would the proper conduct be? I would have on a corset and hoop skirt and bustle and I couldn't even show my ankle, right?

JB. As bad a guy as I'm supposed to be I have to show some kind of breeding, don't I? Some kind of restraint?

HP. Yes, and that of course is written into the play to begin with. You certainly will be charged with dressing a certain way and then will have to move in such a way because of the way you are dressed; your station in society will dictate a lot as well. You are a judge, charged with upholding and interpreting the law— hee, hee!—and in this particular culture in this century, Hedda, sadly there is not much in the way of personal freedom for you being a woman. You know what happened to poor Nora Helmer.

H. So I take the only way out that is left.

HP. Some might say you take a *man's* way out. *Eilert Loborg's* way out. You have been acting 'like a man' for the entire play, playing with guns, aiming them, brandishing them. Your father was a military officer.

H. Right.

HP. Now as to restraint; at this point in rehearsal I would say not at all. You are in *rehearsal;* you are finding the boundaries, either how large or how limited. Then you will seek to fit those choices to the cultural given circumstances of the play. Like King Henry in *Henry the Fifth* says, 'we are the makers of manners.' Because of social status you can do almost whatever you want to do—you *set* those bounds! And as such there is *no need* to show restraint. At this stage in the process I always urge the opposite of restraint; do too much! A play is about people caught up in an outrageous situation caused by love—

JB. Where is the love in this play?

H. Yes! In this play? In this scene?

HP. I'm getting to that. People faced with outrageous situations must make choices just as outrageous in order to fight their way out of those situations; and what could be more outrageous, for a well-born Victorian woman, than to be exposed to scandal with a former lover found dead in the parlor of a Madam, dead of a self-inflicted gunshot wound from the very gun given to him not by the Madam but by that privileged lady? Would that not be outrageous? And in fact, faced with absolutely no alternative but to give in to the slimy clutches of a lascivious judge who has tried to get her into his bed all the time he has known her, is not suicide a viable if not reasonable choice? Is it not an outrageous choice to fit the outrageous situation she is in? The last line of the play is Brack's, who says, upon Tesman's finding her dead, "People don't do such things!" Because normal people would *not do such things* in that society! Ibsen himself has given you the outrageous circumstance and the actions to go with them. You only need to play them fully. And as for love—why not Hedda in a love for Tesman that fell away because of his bookishness that took his attention away from her, a love for excitement—a love for Lovborg? Enough love for him to set him free after she had destroyed his great manuscript in the fire? And Brack—why not, really in his deluded way—*love* for Hedda? Would it not be more interesting to play his affection for Hedda as genuinely love rather than as a bad guy, a blackguard dripping with evil twirling his moustache?

JB. I never thought of it like that. Playing Brack as *genuinely* in love with Hedda?

HP. He can still be a blackguard—and *he is*. It is simply that you the actor are allowing the *audience* to decide that he is a blackguard because of the given circumstances.

JB. What is outrageous for me? My nerve at going after another man's wife?

HP. You have been a so-called 'friend' to Tesman for the entire play, coming to the house to visit, with your real joy and agenda as spending time with Hedda, your real reason for coming. You are trying to have sex—let's just say it flat out—with a married woman, in Victorian Norway! Even though you are a man of position and authority in this society. Is not that outrageous? For Ibsen's audience, fully versed in the mores of the day, it may even be that it was, for them, shocking the way you behaved, seeing it coming, watching you, hearing every allusion, every *double entendre,* every suggestion. For rehearsal I suggest you both begin there and go farther—Brack, take some of the outrageous efforts from the list I gave you: choose to be a snake, or a sloth, or a festering cancer, a poison, a plague, slithering all over her. Try *physically* to slither all over her, all over the room, to engulf her with your slime.

H. Eeeeooww!

HP. And Hedda, who so often is compared to her father, trapped in her petticoats, try to move about and thrash about as if tied up, *trapped* in corset and bustle, struggling, wriggling even if need be on the floor, confined in the dress your society has strapped you into as a woman in this society. Why not even place a gun near you, find a raised shelf to use as a mantel piece, to fight and struggle to get at that gun to use it on him and if not on him, on yourself? Let this become the dynamic of the scene, the both of you tussling, Brack as slime rolling inexorably after you while you roll and inch yourself away from him as best you can, confined in the finery of a lady in good society so frightened of scandal!

H.   Sounds outrageous to me.

JB. Me too.

HP. And let me say one thing more about this play and the 'outrageous choice': in perfecting the climactic structure that is *Hedda Gabler,* does it not already qualify as outrageous for Ibsen to display a gun *center stage* over the mantel piece and insure by the plays' 'Well Made' structure that, merely because it is there, before the end of the final act the gun *must go off?*

### Tips if nothing seems to be happening in your scene:

1. Think less about what you *say* and more about what you *do,* no matter how mundane it might appear to be.

2. Verify that your character *remains in the room and talks with their partner* even though they could well choose to exit.

3. Look for the most outrageous thing—*no matter the context*—your character might say or do instead of their lines or actions as written.

4. Is there the possibility of romantic love—or *visceral hatred*—between you and your scene partner?

5. Always, look for the *antithesis* in the scene.

6. Why does your scene appear in the play at this moment?

# 7. What I have Learned Watching Actors Work

O, Lord, I could have stay'd here all the night
To hear good counsel: O, what learning is!

*Romeo and Juliet*

Over the years I have had the opportunity to watch a lot of actors work, both in rehearsal hall and in the classroom. Here are a few observations I have had, many of which apply both to the audition as well as scene work:

## The First Thing

### Love

It has been said that every play, in one way or another, is about love. Love lost, found, wanted, requited, refused, spurned, gained, missed and longed-for. Even in the dreariest character, you must seek to find in them what is positive and redeemable, what can be loved. No matter how bleak or hopeless a play may seem at first glance—think *Timon of Athens*—keep looking. If the play is worth doing you will find it and at that moment, mark my words, the play will *really* start to click.

# Working with a Scene Partner

## Every Choice Must Make You Need Your Scene Partner

As you begin to work on scenes or monologues you will be making a lot of choices. I want you to make every one of them out of a desire to get closer to your fellow actor; every moment in the scene should make you *need* them more and more. This is true even if your character says, "I want you to leave me alone!" and angrily positions their body away from their scene partner. How can this be? Think of such a line as *sending the other person a message.* Never forget this: as long as the two of you talk with one another longer than a standard greeting and as long as the playwright has not written at the bottom of the page in the stage directions, *gets up and exits,* you can be confident that for some reason you are *meant* to talk to this person, you are meant to be together in the scene. Your objective is about *them* and your action directed toward *them.* You need them! Every moment this is not true is a moment when you do not have a play.

## You Don't Have to Look at Your Scene Partner All the Time!

Allow the needs of a speech to take you away from the other actor's gaze because you are fighting for something outside of you. We do this all the time when we are moved to reminisce with a friend; in effect we 'see' the past memory that we are speaking of—be it pleasant or unpleasant—and cannot help but look back at ourselves how we were then. Because our scene partner is human, too, they will understand. They just might 'see' what we see, as well. This will also satisfy your need, occasionally, to technically cheat out.

## Cheat Out

Young actors are nice people. They believe that it is impolite if you do not look someone in the eye as you talk to them. Being on stage is different; especially if it is a proscenium stage. The audience wants, *needs* to see you in order to understand you. Therefore it is necessary periodically to 'cheat out,' to position yourself in such a way—your director can help with this—that you *appear* to be talking to them and yet your face can still be seen by the audience. Cheating out is also theatrical; what you are saying is so great and profound that the images inherent in it cause you to dream aloud even as you are speaking, even as you are in the throes of reminiscing. In this way you will be able to share the play with the audience, and as an actor on the stage you must be aware of it at all times.

# Director's Notes

## "Less is More"

Of the notes most often abused and misunderstood, few have been more glommed onto than 'Less is more.' "Less is More" only if you can *do* more! Only out of explosion do we as human beings pull back; only when we snap at people do we immediately retreat and attempt to apologize, feeling that we were wrongfully harsh. It is true that the actor cannot dishonestly chew the scenery for the entire play, but it also must be made clear that the very thing which makes less necessary is *doing more*. When directors caution the actor to, "Just be simple. Do less…Simplify." I think what they really mean is *be more specific about what you are fighting for*. Undoubtedly they have just witnessed an actor who does not really know what they want in the scene nor how they are going to fight to get it; lack of specifics makes for wild gestures, over-loud voices and lack of focus. As the actor refines and clarifies exactly what they want in the scene, as they pinpoint the *best* (as well as most exciting) active verb to play to get what they want they will naturally gesture more simply, their voice will modulate better and their focus will be directed where it must always be—their scene partner.

## If You Get a Note about Doing Too Much—*Good!*

If you get a note from the director asking you to 'pull back' or 'tone it down' this is generally a good sign. It means that you are doing exactly what the director wants you to do; you are *working*, bringing to the table choices, ideas, imagination and yes, even talent. You will however need to give it careful consideration because it may also be a sign that in some way you are probably not being as clear or specific as you need to be. As a matter of fact it may be that you are actually not being asked to do less—the director might simply be asking you to do just that; clean up and *clarify* the great big choices you have already brought in.

## "Just *Talk* to Us"

When the director says this they may have seen the actor playing an *attitude* rather than an objective; that is, speaking like they *think* a King would speak rather than playing the objective of *to rule a kingdom, discipline* a servant, in front of the court, for example. They are not asking that you lower your voice to a conversational volume; it may be your character is required in the scene to shout. It has nothing to do with softness or loudness, as it is sometimes misunderstood. The director has heard a dishonest, stereotypical, *unmotivated* line reading which by its nature will make their production look unbelievable and amateurish, and they are asking the actor to do their homework.

## "Over the Top"

The short answer to this of course is that there is no such thing as *"Over the Top."* One of the biggest bones I have to pick with young actors is the question of being large on stage, making the 'big' choice. A play is about unreality; as long as you are true to the play you are acting in and genuinely fighting for something against outrageous odds, it is not possible to drift over the top. This includes your audition monologue. In an audition it will be measured relative to the quiet honest moments you balance it against; sometimes a human being in an outrageous situation—that is, the world of a play—*must* act what appears to be, 'over the top.' It is only when this occurs *all the time* or is not focused upon fighting for an objective that it gets to be "too much."It *is* possible to do more than can be *believed* in a scene, given the style of the play which the director and playwright have established. In this regard it is possible to do "too much." But that has nothing to do with being 'over the top.' Even so-called, "Realistic" plays were not meant to be 'Realistic;' in the end the actor's task is always to make the unbelievable, *believable*.

## A Director's Note to Pick it Up

When a director asks you to 'pick it up' they are not always, of course, asking you to go faster. Ultimately 'pick it up' is about the director wanting you to fight *harder for your objective*. This expediency will give the actor the sound and *appearance* of going faster. And the director will appreciate their production moving along more briskly, as well.

## Louder Faster Funnier

This old theatrical joke is actually, at its core, not a bad note for the actor. Be heard clearly, pick up your cues and raise the stakes as high as possible. This will work for tragedy as well as comedy. It will also make you more professional, as well.

## You Must Earn a Pause

This is an old favorite adage yet it is no less valuable to the actor. If you pause all the time (and the play is not by Harold Pinter) it will lose meaning and slow the play down. But if you briskly pick up your cues—as any actor fighting for their life in an outrageous loving situation should—and then you *suddenly* pause once, it will have meaning.

## Don't Let the Energy Drop and Play the Ends of Words!

You must sustain the energy through the end of the line, because 1: Your character's needs are so great that you must keep on talking and 2: It will be easier for the audience to hear and understand you. We Americans are notorious for dropping sound at the end of a line; unnecessarily softening and getting lazy with the ends of words. Usually we start with a great burst of energy and volume at the *beginning* of the line but because of poor breath control we lose air by the end. Actually the opposite is what is required; the best vocal production gains momentum, with even a slight upward emphasis, by the end of the line. The best way to accomplish this is to hit the consonants; the D's, T's, B's, etc. Clearly bitten ends of words help you be clear on stage, even in the most mumbling, contemporary play. You can get away with hitting them very hard—even harder than you think realistic; to you it may feel exaggerated but to the audience it will actually *sound* conversational. The 'intimate' black box spaces usually don't have a lot of baffling to bounce back the sound and this makes them more deceptive than you might think to project in than the old barns. Also when performing in a black box the actor gets lulled into thinking they can get away with whispering, out of a desire to seem "real."

## Exit

Conversely if you have a false exit—if you attempt to leave the room but are called back or stopped short—*keep walking.* You must get out the door because whatever it is that caused you to want to leave is still driving you. Don't *anticipate* being prevented from going, don't walk just slowly enough for your scene partner to be able to catch up with you. *Make* them stop you from leaving!

## Exit Line

Always hit an exit line a little harder. Because of the fact that you are probably going out of a door, most likely upstage, the audience may lose sight of you and your words. The Exit Line is often of great importance, whether for plot (think of Hamlet's *the play's the thing / Wherein I'll catch the conscience of the king!)* or a capper to the play ("On the contrary, Aunt Augusta, I've now realized for the first time in my life the vital Importance of Being Earnest."). Make sure the audience hears it clearly.

## Explode

You want to display your innate fire and yes, *danger* as an actor. So a carefully—and *strategically*—chosen explosion in your monologue or scene is good and dramatically /dynamically necessary. It may even be written into the scene; the playwright is aware of these varying dynamics, as well. You simply cannot blow up all the time; otherwise it will be meaningless. Once you are aware that an explosion is called for in a scene/speech, look also for the moment when the character is striving to *calm down*. That just may be where even more excitement will come from.

## *Seeming* to Lose Control

As an actor you must never actually lose control; you must seek to *appear* to the eye of the audience that you are losing control. You must never wholly lose control; that is madness. People can get hurt in such situations. Would you do a sword fight with an actor so "into it" they have lost control? This is why for stage combat or dance combinations or anything potentially dangerous you must always warm up and practice them before the show each night. For all of the honesty and 'realism' sought for in the theatre, it is, after all, only an *illusion,* a lie like truth.

## In the Moment

You must be available to react to whatever happens, unplanned, during your monologue or scene, that is you must be *in the moment.* You have not memorized every single reaction (at least not if you are a good actor): you have only memorized your words, your relationship to the people around you and what you want of them.  But during the scene sometimes marvelous, wonderful things that have not been planned before occur and you want to avoid being caught "not listening," or "glassy-eyed," having effectively dropped out of the scene just because you do not have lines. Because of this one of the most difficult roles to play is Shakespearean servant parts. With these roles you must either stand there silent (and alive!) for scene after scene or (worse) you must enter after having been off stage for a long time only to suddenly have to deliver news of earth-shattering importance, such as Seyton must say in *Macbeth:* "The Queen, my lord, is dead." I know. I played Seyton.

# Playing Emotion

## Crying is about Trying *Not* to Cry

This is another old acting chestnut. People do not want to cry; they want to *avoid* crying. But it overtakes them. We are most moved when presented with someone who is doing the very best they can against outrageous odds and *then* are overtaken with emotion; not a wimp who blubbers at the drop of a hat. If you weep once, we are moved; if you cry all the time we don't care and are bored by you.

## Let the *Audience* Do the Feeling

Sometimes actors feel the need to 'help the audience along' when the play gets emotional. They may even try to fain a few sniffles, and tears. Whether actors in doing this realize it or not, this is out of a desire on their part to be *loved by the audience,* to get the audience to feel sorry for them. Please avoid this unprofessional self-indulgence! At emotional moments your character will be engaged as the playwright considers believable for that character, no more or less. If it is not called for you will do well to do what most of us would do in that situation; just 'hang on' as best you can and not get swept away by it. Continue to fight for what you want in a scene and let the chips fall where they may; if emotion comes to you and you fight it most likely even *more* emotion will come. That is what human beings are like. If you feel the need to *show* the audience how emotional you can get, then it just may be you are playing a totally different objective in the play...

# Playing Style

## What You *Wear* Helps You Play Period Style

In classical, period plays think about what you will be wearing as you begin to work on the physicality of your character. Obviously in the plays of Moliere and Wilde there is specific movement and gesture ascribed to people in those cultures, related to the social mores they lived under and *sought to thrive in,* but for you an adjustment in clothing can get you thinking like your character almost at once. A tighter collar, hoop skirt, corset, waistcoat, hard sole shoes, suit jacket will help you get started. In fact you should always attempt to approximate your character's costume in rehearsal; it will save you time getting over that constricted feeling actors get when in costume at dress rehearsal for the first time. And by the way: dressing like your character in rehearsal helps for contemporary plays as well, when you are portraying a person from a different social class than your own.

## Acting with a British Dialect

Too often when young actors appear in a play that requires work with style and dialect—such as *The Importance of Being Earnest, Private Lives*, etc.—the evening becomes about them struggling to wrap their lips around *rehearsed pronunciations* rather than simply portraying human beings living in the work-a-day world who *happen* to speak with a British Dialect. The mistaken notion is that for these plays a "perfect" dialect is required. This may be so for film but I do not believe it is for theatre. For instance if you have ever listened to dialect tapes of real people speaking the Cockney dialect you will realize at once that it is virtually unintelligible to the American ear! Yet this is *perfect.* What is wrong? The problem is that for the stage you must not try to sound perfect; rather you must seek to accurately create the *rhythm* and the *sense* of the dialect. Theatre is about illusion and heightened reality; you only need to successfully portray that which *rings true in the ear* of the audience. Then they will hear what they *believe* to be a 'perfect' dialect. All the actor needs to employ is what we call Standard American Stage Speech, which to our ears today sounds like genuine British because it has the most recognizable sounds, such as the back of the throat a's and soft r's; *AAHH*-unt for **Aunt** and c*AAH*-nt for **can't**, hea-*uh* for **here** and thea-*uh* for **there.** This frees the actor to fight for the character's *needs in the scene* rather than falling for the misguided notion that the show will seem 'fake' to the audience if the actors' dialect isn't 'perfect.' What actually makes actors fake is *not playing the play.* Do not mistake me; if you have a dialect that is word perfect without having to think about it—and you can still be understood by the audience—great. But please remember that these plays are more about those people trying to *survive in that society* rather than how well they substitute diphthongal changes.

## Playing Tennessee Williams

The same mistake is made when approaching the Southern speech found in the works of Tennessee Williams. Too often actors get hung up on this; needlessly they struggle to do what they think is a 'perfect' Southern dialect, thinking the audience will not believe them otherwise. Again, theatre is about *illusion;* any native speech unbridled by the needs of projection and articulation for a live audience can be rendered almost unintelligible. Theatrical convention demands that all dialects must be *adapted to the needs of understandability*, and this means that only a *sense and rhythm* of the speech is required, not perfection. Years ago I directed *Cat on a Hot Tin Roof.* In preparing for auditions I asked the actors not to attempt a southern dialect, and during rehearsal I requested they attempt only a sense of it, at most softening the R's. Why? Because in the first place the actors were all from the Southeastern part of the United States—whether they realized it or not the sound of the south was already in how they spoke— and also because the most important thing was not how those people spoke but rather how they *behaved.* Alma in *Summer and Smoke* would be just as tragic if she spoke with a New England accent as well as southern. As in every play fight for what these people want from each other with all of your soul and heart, and you will be doing the great Tennessee Williams more than justice. Rather than worry so much about a southern dialect, concentrate on playing how *hot the temperature* is in his plays!

## Playing Wilde and Shaw and the Upper Class

F. Scott Fitzgerald said in his 1924 short story *The Rich Boy,* "Let me tell you about the rich. They are different from you and me," but I beg to differ. True they have a tremendous amount of money, they have been born with an enormous amount of privilege and they do not have to give a single thought to what, on a daily basis, we normal folks consider of dire importance: shelter, clothing, food. In this regard they are different. But otherwise they are flesh and blood human beings who like us are sometimes caught up in outrageous situations caused by love; they feel everything as profoundly as we do and need everything we need. When playing the plays of these two great playwrights and plays like them always start with this; what do these characters *want out of life?* You can always add stiff clothing and tilting up the teacup pinky finger *later.*

## Kings and Queens Are Human, Too

In Act V Sc. 2 of Shakespeare's *Henry the Fifth*, King Harry, out of a desire to assure his French bride-to-be that it is quite all right for her to give him a kiss before they are married, says, *"O Kate, nice customs curtsy to great kings. Dear Kate, you and I cannot be confin'd within the weak list of a country's fashion; we are the makers of manners, Kate."* This is instructive for the actor when cast in the role of a king, queen or royalty in general. Too often actors fall into the trap of feeling they have to *show* some kind of carriage or baring to *prove* to the audience that they are kingly. Why not simply look on playing the part of a king in the same way you would play *style?* Approach the role as a human being who just *happens* to have been born into a royal family. There is no need to *indicate* decorum, stature or majesty; there are good kings and bad kings, tall kings and short kings, well bred kings and ill mannered kings. People who are royal, noble or rich who have access to all the best schools and education and privilege the world can provide are just as ill mannered, slovenly and foul as the rest of us commoners are. As a matter of fact, perhaps this privilege and entitlement makes them even *more* so! But all the same we *accept them as a king because they have the crown.* (Just don't forget that even a king had to be *taught* how to walk wearing a crown!) So when playing royalty: underneath that royal crown they are—and *should* be—just as screwed-up as the rest of us are.

## Acting Choices

### To "Get Information" is Not a Good Choice

'How are you today?'
'Fine.'
'Good.'

You have just gotten information. Big deal.

But the play has not been moved forward, has not displayed a single whit of conflict, of outrageous love, of what your character needs or desires most in the world in which they live. Many times, in scenes that seem to be composed of two people 'talking,' student actors name as their character's objective, "To get information." They do not look deeply enough at their scene. They choose what appears to be *on the surface* of what their character is doing, failing to get underneath that action. Suppose you are playing a cop who has been given the task of interrogating a prisoner in a scene. On the face of it you might *appear* to be trying to get information from the prisoner, but careful study of the play will probably lead you in another direction, a direction driven by *subtext.* In your scene there are two things you need to always be aware of; what your character *does* and what is *underneath* what your character does. Take the bulleted list I asked you to make of everything that has happened to your character before the present scene begins. Suppose earlier in the play the prisoner has shot your partner. You might want to get revenge, right? So on the surface it may *appear* that you are interrogating the prisoner but actually you are trying to *exact revenge* against them. Sometimes playwrights employ activities between characters in scenes that might seem outwardly mundane when actually there is great moment and tension inherent in them (Amanda Wingfield mending daughter Laura's dress for her 'gentleman caller,' Gwendolyn and Cecily having tea, Emilia combing Desdemona's hair before bed, Toozenbach having a short passing word with his wife Irina, etc.). Look underneath these moments; a lot more is happening than you might think!

## To "Get Respect" is Not a Good Choice!

To "Get Respect" is another favorite choice of actors in scene work in class. Respect is a good thing but it is not inherently dramatic or interesting. If you do not get it will it mean your death? I mean *really*. Make an acting choice that is *visceral,* that literally involves blood and guts, tears and spit—even if the play is a British drawing room comedy. People in drawing room comedies have tremendous needs, too. When Elyot and Amanda are fighting one another in *Private Lives,* there is no harm if, for only a *second,* they have the desire to kill one another. *Love* is a better objective than *respect.*

## Every Choice Must Be *Visceral.*

Even if there is no possibility of bloodshed in your play, every choice the actor makes should at its core possess the reality that we are all made up of flesh and blood, which, at any moment, *might* be spilt. The desires of the human heart faced with overcoming an outrageous situation can concoct all kinds of fantasies, and not a few of them can result either in horrific violence or, more likely and importantly, the *dream* of horrific violence—or the *fantasy* of a love so everlasting it brings tears to the eyes. Even in the seeming calm inactivity of Chekhov there should be, in the mind of a character caught up in an outrageous situation, the *possibility* of the evening winding up with shed blood (such as Vanya chasing after Serebryakov firing his pistol, Toozenbach marching off to a duel and Ivanov dashing off stage at play's end to shoot himself).

If this bloodshed is accepted as even a possibility—what would you do to avoid it?

## "Kind of" Choices Lead to "Kind of" Acting

You either want what you want or you don't. 'Kind of' is not going to create the world of the play. Nor is 'like,' 'sort of,' 'just,' 'basically.' I have discovered that the word *like* seems to be the contest-winning favorite among my young students (you would be amazed how many times a student can manage to say 'like' when describing aloud what their objective is in a scene). However this does not get them any closer to making a choice that is clear, let alone outrageous. For clarity it is best to decide that a certain thing *is* something rather than *like* something else. 'Like' suggests that you probably have a vague notion close to what you are meaning to express but for some reason you cannot commit. Find out what that true meaning is and do *that*. If your needs are tremendous and rock hard they just might draw a reaction from your scene partner just as rock hard, and maybe even produce real emotion out of the both of you by play's end.

## Do Not Fear 'I Don't Know!'

For the actor who is available to impulse there is a storehouse of possibility in the phrase "I don't know." If you are truly 'in the moment' with your scene partner it can be absolutely thrilling to not know what will happen next. Just don't allow it to become the passive, dead-locked, inactive form of 'I don't know.' Rather let it be the impulsive, energetic, "I DON'T KNOW!" that will cause you to dash about the room seeking answers. This means that, truly, *anything* can happen. The audience feels this thrill, as well.

## Play a Comedy Like a Tragedy...

Play a comedy like a tragedy and a tragedy like a comedy. This is an old theatre tip, I don't know who said it first, but it makes a lot of sense. We laugh at the people of *The Importance of Being Earnest* because they treat the most serious things of life with the most supreme triviality ("And now to minor matters: are your parents living?"). We cry over Willy Loman in *Death of a Salesman* because he took the most trivial things ("be well liked; it's not what you do but who you know") far too seriously. When working on a comedy, look first to how broad and outrageously large you can make the smallest, most meaningless things. Then play that seriousness as if you were Oedipus at Colonus. Or when playing tragedy look for moments in which you can laugh, even be silly; if the play is any good at all both you and the audience are going to need and appreciate those moments.

### Playing Drunk

Drunkenness is, first and foremost, about *loss of inhibition;* you act in a way that you would not act if you were not inebriated. For the actor this works best if you play it as *doing what you always wanted to do but feared reprisal.* This includes loudness and invading another's personal space. The swaying and staggering comes out of dizziness because the drug—and alcohol *is* a drug—has caused blood to rush to your brain, both standing and sitting. Also consider this: people who are drunk *hate to be told* they are drunk! Such an accusation makes them violently angry, affronted, and ready to fight (a fight made impossible, of course, because of their physical impairment). When playing a character who has had too much to drink: speak as loud as possible, seize upon every act which you were afraid of before, take every question as a challenge to fight and get in the face of everyone you talk to. This will help you credibly play 'drunk.' This way you will avoid the phony, stereotypical slurring of words! If you were that drunk you would be rushed to a hospital; if anything you should *over-articulate* your words because you are struggling to prove to the room that you are *not* drunk!

## Technique

### Act *On* the Line

One of the oldest notes in theatre. Actors just starting out are particularly guilty of not doing this. When given a cue they have the habit of physically scrunching up their face before they reply, pausing, reacting *before* they respond. This does not advance the story; it only slows down the play. When in reply react (if you must) *simultaneously as you are replying.* This makes much more sense and best of all keeps the play moving. Your director will appreciate that. Besides, when a friend says something to you that requires a response, how long do *you* wait to reply?

## Your *Real* Cue

Your cue in a scene is not responding to the last word of the person who has just spoken to you; rather it is leaping to defend yourself against something that was said *before* they are finished talking. Example: if someone says to you, "Outside of making you look *fat,* that jacket/dress looks very good on you." You want to angrily reply soon as you hear the word *fat,* right? Not waiting until they are finished talking!

## Always Finish the *Un*-finished Line

Go through your script and find where your character's line ends in an ellipsis (…) or a dash (–). Pencil in what your character was *going to say had they not stopped.* As you rehearse the scene, keep going until your partner stops you. *Make* them stop you; too often actors anticipate being interrupted. This makes for a herky-jerky rhythm to start with and you get into the habit of *expecting* to hear a certain line—or worse, certain line reading. Always keep going when the scene has you in a false stop. Perhaps you will end up overlapping your partner, which at worst will keep the scene moving and at best will help you find even more energy and drive and chances to make outrageous choices. And because your partner gets in the habit of being interrupted it will likely raise their temperature, as well.

## Playing Age

In these times in which age-appropriate casting is the fashion, the instance of young actors judiciously applying dark grease paint marks to their face for wrinkles and white shoe polish in their hair to play age is very rare.  I am sad to see this go; I want the young actor in training to experience every inch of the demands of theatrical magic.  That said, if by chance you do find yourself in the position of being cast as a character in, say, their 60's or 70's or even older, consider this; what will age you most to the eye of the audience is *economy of movement.* Young folks constantly shift from left leg to right leg, they wave their arms, fidget and cannot seem to stop moving.  Old folks have been there and done that; they are slowing down, having fought all the battles, and wish to take it easy while like Lear they "crawl toward death." This is especially true of gesturing with your hands; where you might be tempted to point with your finger three times cut it down to one; where you might normally plop yourself down in a chair with youthful abandon try to lower yourself gradually lest a hip might break. As you are sitting still be extremely sparing in movement or gestures of any kind; you will be surprised how aged—and how *powerful*—you can look when you do not move at all.

## When a Character Makes Up Sounds and Words

In the Gentleman Caller's speech to Laura in *The Glass Menagerie* there is a moment when he tries to encourage her, to cajole her out of her dumps by illustrating how exciting the future will be in the mechanized, coming space age. He shouts aloud, making sounds of jet planes taking off, explosions in the air, stars streaking across the sky. The way to play these words is to *over-emphasize* them, not pull back from them.  Shakespeare made up some 17,000 words because he could not think of one to express what he wanted to say; the character's needs were so great they *defied definition.* Yet these characters had to speak anyway! This is true of Jim speaking to Laura as he fights to explain to her his need to be somebody someday.  It is also the same thing we do every day when we are somehow moved to shout, "fudge," "dag nabbit!"

or "Fiddle Faddle!"(Or worse!) We may not have the right words to express our feelings but we are exasperated to the point that we must speak anyway and so we even make up words if we have to! Such words by their nature *beg* to be over-emphasized!

## Don't Look Down for Too Long—Even Into a Grave.

This is akin to my note "Up Good Down Bad" which I speak about in greater detail in the next part. The actors in the Requiem in *Death of a Salesman* are indeed at the gravesite of Willy Loman, but in addition to his grave they are looking into the *past* as well as the *future*. The audience still needs to see your face, still wants to 'hear' the story which is aided by seeing your expression, and the play still must be shared with them. Of course you will be spending more time than usual looking down to the stage in a scene at a gravesite; but try to, yes, *cheat up* as much as possible. We in the audience will still believe you are at a gravesite.

## Hold for Laugh

Even though you must hold for laughter after a funny punch line in a comedy you are not ceasing to be in the play. All of those seconds you are waiting for the crest of the laugh to just begin to start downward (which is when you speak again) you should still be reacting, still energized, focused, concentrated. It is a stage convention we accept that you are moved to halt, not because you are allowing your audience to laugh (although that is exactly what you are doing), but because your character is so deeply caught up in the moment that you need a 'breather' to figure out the best attack to take next. Try thinking of it that way.

## Stage Whisper

Try to avoid actually whispering. It is bad for your throat. Think of a 'stage whisper' as *the desire to keep from being overheard.* This way you can speak with virtually your full voice—the audience will accept this theatrical convention; they do it all the time in classical plays—and you will still be *believed* to be 'whispering.'

### Playing a Hero When You are *Supposed* to be a Hero

My thoughts on this are similar to the adage, "Play a Tragedy like a Comedy and a Comedy like a Tragedy." Unless you are in a Melodrama you will want to look for the opposites in a character, his or her complexity. Only in comic books are heroes and heroines flawless; the rest of us in the audience are most moved by that character who is just like us—that is, they have faults, they mess up, they *fail*—and yet in spite of this constant failure, when the going gets tough, they are *somehow* able to show courage; they are able to rise above their lesser nature and do something we call *heroic*. For Oedipus, Antigone, the Count of Monte Cristo, John Proctor in *The Crucible,* Thomas More in *A Man for All Seasons*, Saint Joan (both from Anouilh as well as Shaw), Prince Hal and many more heroes and heroines, seek the richness in these characters so that the audience will not be bored for three hours by someone who is a "hero" or a "saint." Seek to play their weakness, their vulnerability; for Saint Joan help us see a young country girl's *fear of death* on the stake; for Saint Thomas More make him *question* his piety and faith; for John Proctor make him *desperate* to confess to Judge Danforth—as long as he does not have to 'sign his name.' These are the acts of human beings *called* to heroism, not born to it, and we are moved to tears by them because we are not sure we could do the same thing if in their place.

## Working on the Script in Rehearsal

### But I Can't Do *That* Because My Line Says *This!*

"I love you" doesn't have to be said 'lovingly' any more than "I hate you" has to be said hatefully! This is what is known as *irony*. It may well be that the playwright wants you to speak it in the traditional way, but you are in rehearsal, right? See what happens if you try something outrageous. Play an argument as a love scene and a love scene as a knock down drag out fight (like Elyot and Amanda in *Private Lives*). Who knows? You just might make an exciting discovery.

## You Must Meet the Play on *its* Terms

Sometimes when actors work on a pre-twentieth century period piece, such as *Hedda Gabler* or *Tartuffe* or *The Importance of Being Earnest,* etc. they forget that it has been written in a different time, place and culture. Rightfully they seek to play actions to win objectives and they recognize that those characters they are trying to play from so long ago are flesh and blood imperfect human beings just like them. But they then make the mistake of allowing their new millennium value judgments to sneak into the discussion. These plays must be approached not only as if you were a human being bound to do what that playwright decreed you must do, they must also be accepted as happening in a circumstance perhaps far removed from your own. This is where research comes in. It is true that you must always *do* what the character does, but you must understand that you are also doing it in the *manner* which they are doing it because of the unique *society* in which they lived and hoped to thrive. Hence Hedda is forced to an outrageous act (suicide) for a very logical and societal reason—the avoidance of scandal; Othello commits murder rather than suing for divorce because being a Moor his honor is at the center of his culture; in Moliere's time men "made a leg" in front of women to show sexual attractiveness; before the 20th Century women were only allowed to show their ankles in public; in Victorian England people wore tighter, more constricting clothing—no doubt to make it that much harder to take the clothes *off* in sudden fits of lust! The actor's imagination is tasked not only with coming up with exciting active verbs to play; it also takes effort to remember—and study—the kind of play you are acting in.

# "Do You Think I'm Any Good?"

## The Question of Talent

I should probably say a word about Talent. In my view the question of whether or not you have Talent is, as Hamlet would have said, "where madness lies." I have not spoken about this before now because I simply feel it is less important than any of the other things I have spoken about. Yes; *any* of the other things. In speaking to you it is my assumption that you have talent—or at least you *think* you do. Talent is a wonderful thing, but as you will find if you continue in the biz, it is not the most important thing, at least not immediately. Do not get me wrong; I believe that in order to succeed an actor must have talent. It is important, but it is also *ephemeral*; it seems that almost no two people can agree upon it or define it. Yet the question can drive young actors to tears and distraction. I do not want you to give the question of "Am I Any Good?" another thought. There are so many variables in the process of acting that I think the young performer will be served best by simply working like hell at what is *within* their control— training in voice and diction, singing, movement, text analysis, self-acceptance and *self-love*. If you press me I will have to come down on the side of being *right* for a role as more important than being *talented*. I say this because directors, when viewing actors in audition, first concern themselves with, "Is this actor right for the role I am casting?" It is after they have decided, "Yes, this actor is right for the role," that they can afford to ask themselves, "Are they talented enough to play the part?" If that question can be answered in the affirmative, then you get cast.

But please consider: An actor can be so right that the director—in their director's *hubris*—thinks, "This actor is not as good as I'd like but they are so *right* for the part I know that I can work with them. I can *coach this actor through* the role." The value of Type is that important. On the other hand it is entirely possible that a director will say, "This actor isn't quite the right type but they are so good that I simply have to use them. I want them in my show!" This is what you are hoping every single time you go to an audition; that your talent will trump the director's notion of the kind of actor they need to play a part. In fact, this is the age-old plea of every actor who enters the profession; "Just give me a chance and I'll show you how good I am!" That is also why I insist on you injecting the outrageous into your work, which might make you more persuasive in the audition situation thanks to your fearlessness.

So what then can we finally say is talent? What is 'Good?' What is bad? Who should be the judge of whether you are a good actor or a bad actor? The simplest answer to this is *you* should be. The director's task is finding the people who are right for the roles first; then they will take up the question of whether or not that person is a good actor. Therefore let me ask you; if you were deemed to be 'not any good,' would that stop you? *Should* it stop you? I propose to set you free from the tyranny of an outsider's words: why don't you, right now, simply say, aloud, "All right. I am NOT any good as an actor! But I am *STILL* going to have a *career* as an actor!" What could be more liberating and ultimately more empowering than to fully embrace the idea that you do not possess the talent to make it as an actor and *yet* by *an act of will* you remain determined that you will still make it as an actor? Is not that a more realistic, more mature way to look at it? In this regard no acting teacher, no director, no theatrical agent can harm you anymore, you will be impervious to their criticism. If you just *accept the possibility of being **un-**talented you are then free to actually **be** talented!*

I admit that this may take some getting used to. After all that I have said, I still believe in talent; talent is a wonderful thing and it is truly joyous to behold. I just don't want it to get in the way of you doing your work. To be fair and perfectly candid, no amount of will is going to help you have a career if at the end of the day you are never cast; if you truly want a gauge of success it is being *cast*—maybe not in the role you want or think you ought to have, but by getting into a show *somehow*. If this does not materialize for you in some good measure—if you never work and never get into the show in at least some kind of role—I would say then that the handwriting is on the wall. But for now I don't want you to waste your time, your blood, sweat and tears obsessing about it. I want you to work harder at learning to fight for what you want against unbelievable odds in *life* as well as in a play. The question of talent will take care of itself.

---

## *Summary of Part One*

1.  *A play is about people caught up in an Outrageous situation, caused by Love.*

2.  *Actors must make choices to match the outrageous situations in a play.*

3.  *In rehearsal it is helpful to make these choices, even if at first they do not fit the play.*

4.  *It is extremely important that the actor choose an active verb which incites them to do something.*

5.  *The actor should concentrate on doing what the playwright has written their character does, not about whether or not they themselves would do it in that circumstance.*

6.  *Even in the quietest scenes there is the possibility of outrageous action between characters.*

7.  *If the playwright has not written EXIT as a stage direction the actor can be confident that they must engage the other person in the scene.*

8.  *Play emotion as a series of actions, not as a condition that has come over you.*

9.  *Actors must always look for the love in their character and in the play.*

---

# Part Two: Working on Monologues

"I warrant thee; if I do not act it, hiss me."

*The Merry Wives of Windsor*

# 8. What a Monologue Is

## Mono·logue

*noun* \\'mä-nə-,lȯg, -,läg\\

**1:** A dramatic soliloquy; *also* a dramatic sketch performed by one actor

## So·lil·o·quy

*noun* \\sə-' li-lə-kwē\\
**1:** The act of talking to oneself
**2:** A dramatic monologue that gives the illusion of being a series of unspoken reflections

*Webster's New Collegiate Dictionary, 1977*

We have spoken about how a play is about human beings caught up in outrageous situations caused by love, and that as an actor you need to make bigger, bolder, more outrageous choices to match. We have said that these choices can enliven and enrich your work and make you more hirable as an actor because you are able to present to the director an actor who is open, available, fearless and imaginative and yes, possibly, even *talented.*

Just as important, and perhaps even more so, is making these same outrageous choices in the audition. The difference here is that the outrageous situation is doubled—it counts for the world of the play *and* the audition itself. That is, you are serving two masters; the Big Choice both as the *character* and *actor;* the character making outrageous choices against outrageous situations *in the play* and the actor making outrageous choices in that material as a *vehicle to get a job.* Please keep this thought fast near your heart as you proceed.

## Monologues and Soliloquies

A monologue is a long speech usually spoken from one character to another, but it can also be spoken by oneself. A soliloquy is always spoken when the character is alone. Whether monologue or soliloquy recognize that the "long speech" comes out of some great need *within the heart of the speaker.* I would like to suggest this:

- A soliloquy is never spoken *to* yourself (apology to Webster).

- A long speech is spoken out loud as a desire to fight for something *outside* of oneself, a need too great and far away to be reached otherwise. You are fighting to find an answer to some awesome question that has eluded you, gotten away from you. You can say that a monologue is about discovering the *outrageous truth.*

- A monologue is a monologue—that is, you keep on talking—because you discover in the midst of it that there *is much more to say!* With every succeeding line, a long speech is a *discovery* you are only now able to see!

- This discovery grows more dire or *glorious* the longer it goes on; therefore it must build as you get toward the end. Imagine returning home after a long journey and seeing your house come gradually into focus; do you not slowly begin to pick up speed and are perhaps sprinting by the time you bound up the steps to return to your beloved front door?

- In Shakespeare you are perfectly free to speak directly to the audience; in a contemporary play if the speech is by yourself you must speak to the fourth wall. (Or to the EXIT sign in the back of the auditorium). However, whether realistic or presentational, your character's desire must be in effect to burst *through* that fourth wall in front of you; your human need must be that great.

A play is about people caught up in an outrageous situation caused by love. In a long speech *your words* are fighting through that outrageous situation. In the midst of the equally outrageous situation known as the audition your weapon is still the spoken word only in this case it is the *audition* that is your obstacle, what you are fighting your way through to *get a job.*

## Monologues to Study

Here are a few examples of work on speeches you might do for an audition. I have tried to list potential problem spots with each of them—that is, pitfalls you might be in danger of falling into when attempting them—and I have listed a few outrageous actions which might fit the needs of believability as well as theatricality.

### The Rainmaker by N. Richard Nash:

### Starbuck

In this speech Bill Starbuck is forced to confront the spinster Lizzie Curry. He angrily challenges her harsh misjudgment of him, her sneering at his way of life and the notion that he can bring rain. This scene, which is in Act 2, ends with him disgusted with her for not being able to believe what she cannot see, but by the end of the act Starbuck has made it possible for her to see and believe much more.

As I work with an actor on a monologue I begin, as always, with:

"Who are you talking to?"

STARBUCK. Lizzie.

HP. What do you want from her? Right now?

S. I want her respect.

HP. Just her respect?

S. Yes; she has treated me badly, accused me of lying, being a criminal...

HP. So you want her respect. What will you do when you get it?

S. When I get it...?

HP. How great will it be for this country spinster to respect you?

S. Well...

HP. If she doesn't wind up respecting you, what then? What bad will happen?

S. Bad?

HP. What awful thing will happen to you? If you must have her respect that badly.

S. Well...

HP. Is there a chance that you want something else from her? Here and now?

S. Here and now? You mean right here and now? In this scene?

HP. Yep. In this scene. The next scene has not happened yet so it doesn't matter what you think of that. What has happened before this scene? All the scenes in which you appeared, in which you appeared with her?

S. I—greeted her, complimented her...

HP. What else?

S. I told her how—beautiful she is—that she is *pretty*—later in the scene.

HP. Right. Now you are alone here on the farm, in the farmhouse. All of her brothers are in town gallivanting, maybe with women. You and Lizzie are left here on the farm, all by yourselves. Whatever happens after this scene does not matter; you want to make a choice that is here and now and in this moment, fed by all that has gone on between the two of you before. What do you want from her?

S. I want her to—like me?

HP. Much better. How do you do that? What do you *do* to get her to do that? To get her to like you?

S. I—yell at her? No, that's not right…

HP. Try again. It's questionable if yelling at someone will get them to like you. And besides you can only yell for so long; your voice might give out.

S. I—treat her nice? But I seem to be mad at her—

HP. First things first. And by the way "be mad" is a state of being, which you cannot play. Let me help you. How about the active verb, "to woo?" How about *wooing* her?

S. That sounds good but I start the speech by—

HP. Yes, you shout at her, yell at her. Now of course there are a lot of ways to say those lines, a lot of attitudes and subtext you can bring to the speech. And of course your tactics can change during the scene. Suppose you want to woo her but first you must 'get her attention?'

S. Get her attention?

HP. And you choose to do this by shouting her down; yelling at her. Under those circumstances yelling at her is not such a bad thing. All of these are active verbs. Remember if you make the choice that you are yelling at her it is not because of who she is but how she has been *behaving.* You know how sometimes people who are getting hysterical are slapped on the face to actually *calm them down?* There is a difference there. Once you have done this—that is, once she has heard you and quieted herself—you can then go about your objective of getting her to like you. Let's look at the body of the speech where you talk about your brothers; they had such great jobs, one a doctor and one a singer with a beautiful voice, but they could do nothing about the drought. But you—

S. Me—?

HP. Remember? You told her you went off and you called for rain, and it came! During this part of the speech can you bring an image to mind? You are being big and brash and bragging in this section—yes I know I'm speaking in terms of qualities; ignore them!—what do you think such a person who does that might be like? What kind of job might you have? One that works on Sunday, let's say…?

S. A preacher?

HP. Exactly! A preacher. You are similar to a preacher, to an evangelist, and you know how they act, so big and bombastic and charismatic? What I just listed are qualities of course but you get the idea; you *do* something to produce the impression of these qualities in the minds of the audience. What an evangelist *does.* What verbs might we come up with to get to those qualities?

S. Preach? Proselytize?

HP. I like preach better. How about a few more? How about to celebrate? To exalt? To praise? To revere? To worship? To proclaim? To open up—as in, 'their eyes'?

S. All those? To get her to like me?

HP. Remember your tactic can change. Over and over. If you win her to your 'faith' she might be impressed enough with *your* amazing faith to like you. If she can like you then she can let down her guard; if she lets down her guard then you can appeal to her as man to woman, and *then*...

S. I can go through that many changes?

HP. Of course you can. You're a human being in an outrageous situation; you don't have a choice. Let me ask you something else. Do you think you planned to make love to her?

S. Yes; Starbuck is a salesman, a Rainmaker...

HP. Isn't that calculating? A little too much thinking ahead?

S. Well. He came into town trying to sell--

HP. How about if he wanted to open a brave new world to her and *in the moment* fell for her? Isn't that more interesting? That way she can take him on a journey, too. See how that might be more human?

S. It makes him—me—more open, how you like to say – *available.*

HP. Very good. And another thing: perhaps Starbuck needs to make Lizzie believe that she is pretty in order for himself to believe that he can bring rain? Maybe he is not convinced at all in himself? That gives him a journey to go through, doesn't it?

S. I never thought of it that way; he seems so loud, so confident...

HP. Maybe that loud confidence *is a mask he wears to cover up his lack of confidence!* Also one more thing, to make it more outrageous…

S. What's that?

HP. At the end of your speech, when you've convinced her of the honor of your family and your amazing faith and talent to bring rain, do this: raise your arms to the sky and scream "Hallelujah" to the top of your voice!

**Pitfall of this speech:** Being too big, playing too much of the bombastic ringleader, shouting on one calculating level.

**Solution for it:** Vulnerability; allow Starbuck to go through a journey as well as taking Lizzie on one; he has not planned everything; he is not certain that she will buy his story, he is not certain that he can bring rain, he has to be convinced of his ability just as much as she does that she is pretty; if she doesn't believe him what then?

## Summer and Smoke by Tennessee Williams:

### Alma

This monologue, near the end of the play, is quite useful for the unified, 60-second audition but it has the pitfall of easily becoming whiny and playing on the one level of "I'm a loser!" It is a speech which will definitely benefit from playing the "Big Two": Love and Antithesis. The actress working on it wants to:

- Play the obvious, unrequited love in the speech but must not fall into the trap of going for the weak, soppy, "I've failed!" kind of love. Play rather the love that is pure, glorious, and *never happened; the hoped for love* she had for John. The love that eludes us is every bit as powerful as the love we possessed because it is made up of *imagined* dreams, aspirations and fantasies without the cold reality of what actually happened. In this way Alma comes across as hopeful and we pull for her because she has not already decided by her actions and attitude that she is a loser!

- Even a loser will not applaud another loser. The audience cheers and cries for a human being just like them; that is, one that does their best against admittedly impossible odds and yet ultimately fails. The moment you feel sorry for yourself, the moment that you cry *first*...! Forget about it.

- Play the Antithesis. Yes, our Shakespearean word for 'opposites,' again. Monologues must never be presented on one level, even if they fit the category of actually *being* on one level, such as, "angry," or "funny," or, "quiet." Though the speech is short, Alma must find as much upbeat, happy joy within it as she can. During this sad, giving-up farewell to the only man she ever loved she must even find a spot where she can laugh out loud with the excitement and love of the good times in their past! A good place to try this is when she is describing how she watched him next door from inside her window. This should be so pleasant, so genuinely loving and so happy that she had at least *that* memory of him, that we are shocked when the speech ends so unhappily.

**Pitfall:** Playing the loser; playing the despair of it being over and hopeless with John.

**Solution:** Fighting for his love even now; not accepting that it is hopeless; genuinely enjoying and seeing again the wonderful memories of being his next-door neighbor as a child; love is still possible! All is not lost!

# Hamlet by William Shakespeare:

## Hamlet

### "To be, or not to be..."

You are not likely to see this famous speech at an audition, and you are well advised to avoid it yourself. It is simply too famous, too known by everyone you are likely to audition for; probably most people who are in theatre have at least some idea about what this speech is about, how they might do it, how it ought to be done by others, and most likely none of these people will agree. This is one of those sacred, cherished pieces of dramatic literature so untouchable in its reverence you are in danger of not actually being heard doing it; listeners will be hearing *themselves* speaking, taken away into their own thoughts about life and art, far away from you. Yet of course productions of it are done somewhere every year, perhaps every day, across the globe. Tread softly if you are considering this monumentally heavy lift. Besides, the auditor might rightly ask, "If you are good enough to do Hamlet why can't you find another speech *I haven't heard before that does the same thing*?" This is a good point.

However it is still useful to explore the speech in order to touch upon a few helpful thoughts when doing Shakespeare that you can relate to other speeches.

- I see this speech as fighting *to live* rather than choosing to *die*. (Notice the *antithesis*.)

- Do not fall into the trap of being introspective or brooding. This is one of the most common mistakes made with this soliloquy. The actor gets caught up in *playing the idea* of Hamlet, caught up in the madness he feigns, the vengeance he seeks, the love for Ophelia, all of his youthful *sturm und drang*. Speaking this speech out loud is not therapy; it is *fighting* to decide which is better, life or death?

- Give in to what Shakespeare has given you, the *words,* to strike out and hit back. Hamlet is fighting, wrestling, stabbing at death itself; the speech—as every soliloquy—is about crying out rather than suffering from within. The only thing certain is that life on this 'mortal coil' is far too short—but just the same *baring it,* with those 'ills we have,' is still far better than that 'undiscover'd country from whose bourn no traveler returns.'

- It is about *love of life* rather than *fear of death!*

Try it on for size to see what I mean:

To be, or not to be: that is the question:
Whether 'tis nobler in the mind to suffer
The slings and arrows of outrageous fortune,
Or to take arms against a sea of troubles,
And by opposing end them? To die: to sleep;
No more; and by a sleep to say we end
The heart-ache and the thousand natural shocks
That flesh is heir to, 'tis a consummation
Devoutly to be wish'd. To die, to sleep;
To sleep: perchance to dream: ay, there's the rub;
For in that sleep of death what dreams may come
When we have shuffled off this mortal coil,
Must give us pause: there's the respect
That makes calamity of so long life;
For who would bear the whips and scorns of time,
The oppressor's wrong, the proud man's contumely,
The pangs of despised love, the law's delay,
The insolence of office and the spurns
That patient merit of the unworthy takes,
When he himself might his quietus make
With a bare bodkin? who would fardels bear,
To grunt and sweat under a weary life,
But that the dread of something after death,
The undiscover'd country from whose bourn
No traveller returns, puzzles the will

And makes us rather bear those ills we have
Than fly to others that we know not of?
Thus conscience does make cowards of us all;
And thus the native hue of resolution
Is sicklied o'er with the pale cast of thought,
And enterprises of great pith and moment
With this regard their currents turn awry,
And lose the name of action.--Soft you now!
The fair Ophelia! Nymph, in thy orisons
Be all my sins remember'd.

**Pitfall:** It's *Hamlet*. The danger is playing the gloom and doom of Hamlet's grief and confusion over the appearance of his father's ghost. There is also the self-conscious fear of not doing justice to perhaps the greatest speech in the history of the English language.

**Solution:** It's *Shakespeare's* Hamlet. This means there are countless images to play in his words; many allusions, both positive and negative, to present to the audience; actively fighting to live rather than giving up and committing suicide; playing the resolution at the end of the speech as a triumph filled with hope rather than a poor consolation prize to keep on living. And by the way: a most excellent example of antithesis is the first line of the speech!

### Hamlet:

### Ophelia

### "O, what a noble mind is here o'erthrown!"

Almost as challenging is this speech of Ophelia, which follows Hamlet's wild 'get thee to a nunnery' tirade. Of course there is the pitfall of playing only horror, spurned love, disappointment, fear of his madness. But as usual Shakespeare has given you, even in this short speech, so much more to do.

I talk to the actress playing the part:

HP. Who are you talking to?

OPHELIA. Myself—no—

HP. Ah! You caught yourself!

OPH. Sorry. To the *audience*; to something *outside* of myself.

HP. Good job. What do you want?

OPHELIA. I want Hamlet.

HP. True; in the long run. What do you want in *this* moment?

OPH. I want to show the audience how desperate he has made me.

HP. Show? How do you show them that?

OPH. By looking at them, pleading to them…

HP. What do you get if you are successful in showing them your desperation?

OPH. They will sympathize with me.

HP. Why do they need to do that?

OPH. Because I am—*Ophelia;* I have just been attacked by Hamlet—

HP. So they might cry a little when you go mad and die later?

OPH. Well…

HP. How about we choose something besides 'show?'

OPH. You asked me what I wanted.

HP. Yes; in *this* moment, after he has gone.

OPH. How about—sympathy?

HP. Okay. From—the audience?

OPH. Yes.

HP. And what is so great about that?

OPH. I feel better if they…feel sorry for me.

HP. What do you tell them?

OPH. I say, 'O woe is me—'

HP. You don't say that until the end of the speech. You say a lot of stuff, directly to the audience, before you get to that. What do you say to them first?

OPH. I say—

HP. Do the speech. Let's hear the speech.

OPH.   O, what a noble mind is here o'erthrown!
    The courtier's, soldier's, scholar's, eye, tongue, sword;
    The expectancy and rose of the fair state,
    The glass of fashion and the mould of form,
    The observed of all observers, quite, quite down!
    And I, of ladies most deject and wretched,
    That suck'd the honey of his music vows,
    Now see that noble and most sovereign reason,
    Like sweet bells jangled, out of tune and harsh;
    That unmatch'd form and feature of blown youth
    Blasted with ecstasy: O, woe is me,
    To have seen what I have seen, see what I see!

HP. What do you say about him?

OPH. I say that I am sorry he—

HP. Has gone crazy—

OPH.—yes, he has gone crazy; then I describe how much he is loved in the country—

HP. He is quite loved by the people isn't he? Been given a lot of breeding and education, right? He is heir to the throne, highly thought of, well brought up—

OPH. And he has gone crazy.

HP. He has fallen. Right? The 'observed of all observers—

OPH. 'Quite, quite down,' yes. He has fallen badly.

HP. And what about you?

OPH. I 'sucked the honey of his music vows—'

HP. You fell in love with him. You believed his poems. And now—

OPH. 'Now see that noble and most sovereign reason, / Like sweet bells jangled, out of tune and harsh.'

HP. And then what?

OPH. 'That unmatch'd form and feature of blown youth / Blasted with ecstasy O, woe is me, / To have seen what I have seen, see what I see!'

HP. You finally get to yourself. Yes, you are now woeful; but Shakespeare has kept you from mentioning it until the very end. What does that tell you about the speech?

OPH. That I am sorrier for Hamlet's fall than I am for my woe in seeing it?

HP. That is what love is, isn't it?

OPH. Oh…Yes. So I am telling the audience how bad it is that Hamlet has gone mad?

HP. Think of a different active verb than 'tell.'

OPH. To—proclaim. To—Pronounce. To—

HP. More personal.

OPH. Lament.

HP. That's more like it.

OPH. Lament. Cry. Wail.

HP. How about blubber? Does that make you think of something to do?

OPH. Yes; crying like a baby.

HP. Or at least as *helpless* as a baby. And how about moan? Yowl? Keen? Like the Irish do at a funeral.

OPH. That makes me think of *mourn,* as well. Does that work?

HP. Yes. You are mourning Hamlet's 'passing' to the audience and thereby *showing them how much you love him.* Of course those are not the only choices.

OPH. Got it. Thanks.

HP. Also—don't forget to play the antithesis in the speech; '*sweet bells jangled, blasted* with *ecstasy.'* Suppose, to play the outrageous, you suddenly *become* those sweet bells, jangled, out of tune and harsh?

OPH. Oh my! Wouldn't that be too much?

HP. What's 'too much?' If you are in the midst of an outrageous situation caused by love, which you are, you are capable of anything! True you are not actually becoming those bells but the bells are very instructive—Shakespeare is very instructive, in helping you speak the speech. Try it out as an improv; the next time you do the speech, sound out like a sweet bell as you begin talking, then gradually jangle, jingle jangle, slowly losing the proper tune, going off key, then getting a-tonal, then much more harsh, and let this take you past 'O woe is me!' through to the end of the speech. Try that and see what happens to you.

OPH. So in the speech am I saying that, *Hamlet and I both* are sweet bells jangled out of tune and harsh?!

HP. You got it! Excellent! Shakespeare has given you these wonderful metaphors to play. You can choose to play them physically or you can let the images become *given circumstances* which are driving you *inside*. Acting out the sounds of the jangled bells only needs to free you so that you will be available to the real, organic impulses that want to come over you after you have done the crazy act of making bell sounds off key! Remember how I always talk about how you should really take note of the 'come down' after the 'blow up?' This is the same thing. And it is that come down that Ophelia is going through, for the entire speech, after Hamlet has left her. This is the horrible grief she feels: Hamlet becoming a 'jangled tune' because of his perceived madness and she a 'jangled tune' because of losing his love! The line 'O woe is me!' makes perfect sense because we get *why* you are so woeful, without your needing at all to *show* us you are woeful.

**Pitfall:** It's Ophelia. Playing the victim; playing the classic ingénue damsel in distress; playing too early that she will one day go mad; feeling sorry for herself.

**Solution:** Play the greater sorrow for Hamlet. Lament to the audience the sorrow of what he has lost, how high he was raised and how far he has fallen; using this as a metaphor for yourself; playing the images Shakespeare has given you in the speech; taking the risk of becoming a 'sweet bell jangled out of tune and harsh.'

### The Iceman Cometh by Eugene O'Neill:

### Joe Mott

I have used this monologue for auditions for many years and I admit that I too refer to it as my "Angry Black Man" speech. It comes in the middle of Act Three.

I talk to *myself* about it:

HERB PARKER. So this is your 'Angry Black Man' speech?

HERB PARKER. Yes. Been using it for 30 years.

HP. Who are you talking to?

HP. Everybody in Harry Hope's flophouse bar.

HP. What do you want?

HP. I want their love.

HP. Good choice. Love as a stronger choice than, say, *respect?*

HP. Yes.

HP. Now is this love in this moment, or for the life of the play?

HP. Oh; sorry. You got me there. The love is for the entire play. For this scene I want them shamed; I want to punish them for treating me like dirt because I am black. I must *tell them off* in order to get this.

HP. What possible pitfalls do you see in this speech?

HP. Aren't you going to ask me why I choose it? What it can afford me in the way of contrast?

HP. I already know that; you are African American, and most of the work you have been hired to do is language based and classical; you speak well, with resonance; you are a character actor so you are going to play any host of classical stock characters that run around in those old plays. So you need something to balance that; to say, 'I am also of *today* in my work; I can do contemporary plays, as well; ethnic plays, *Black* plays.

HP. You got it.

HP. But the pitfall of this speech is—?

HP.—the possibility of it being on one level; just yelling and mad.

HP. Right. So what do you do to avoid that?

HP. I laugh and celebrate the possibility of opening my old gambling house for colored men. I brag and laugh about being a 'gamblin'' man—which of course I am clearly not very good at because I am staying in the flophouse and drink all day. But I laugh and prance and boast in the middle of the speech, as a beat of showing them I am not afraid to leave them—though of course I am. This reality leads me back to the fact that I actually *have* to walk out, so I had better make it look good by hurling a bit more vitriol at them as I go out the door.

HP. The 'vitriol' seems to bookend the way you do the speech.

HP. It does, as a matter of fact.

HP. Nicely done, if I say so myself.

HP. Thank you.

HP. You start 'mad,' 'celebrate' and 'boast,' maybe even laugh out loud for good measure in the middle for a good beat change, then tell them off one more time as you go out the door.

HP. I hope it reads that way.

HP. One other thing to help you avoid the one level of 'Angry Black Man.'

HP. Yes?

HP. Don't forget to find the *love* in the speech. Joe has a great deal of affection for Harry Hope and Hickey and in fact all of the gang in the flophouse, being the only Negro there. See next time if you can eke out even a moment of genuine love as a barrier to your yelling at them, leaving the bar.

HP. That's a good idea.

HP. I thought you'd like it.

**Pitfall:** You know it so well you think you know it all and that you have made all of the discoveries. It can become one level of 'angry black guy' yelling at a roomful of white people (not unlike the roomful of people the actor will actually be auditioning for!).

**Solution:** Play the love for all the inhabitants of Harry Hope's flophouse. Play not wanting to leave them. Play the joy and pride of opening up your old gambling house again, the pleasure of being such a great gambler and crap shooter (even though you were never this; you are merely allowing the fantasy to *overtake* you).

## The Glass Menagerie by Tennessee Williams:

## Tom Act 1, Sc. 6

This speech is both a memory and a metaphor. In speaking about the world waiting for "bombardments," Tom is alluding to the coming World War and the coming Gentleman Caller. Because he is talking about a memory of life during summer, with music wafting from the nearby Paradise Dance Hall, there is the danger that the speech can quickly become a *mood* piece; driven not by action so much as imagery. To a degree I actually think this might be Williams' intention, but of course your acting choice must be active rather than a state of being, you must discover what you do rather than feel, such as, perhaps, warning the listener about the *horror life can bring*. Tom may have even seen such horror as he travelled the world, and he relates it to despair and hopelessness— perhaps the despair and hopelessness he saw in Laura's and his mother's eyes when Jim left the apartment to pick up his fiancée.'

How about these possibilities:

- Even if it seems to be written that way, avoid playing the speech as a pastoral, image-driven reminiscence. Think always in terms of speaking out of a desire to *do and incite* rather than to *remember*. Better yet, to do and incite *because* you have remembered something.

- Make choices that are aggressive; do not let the imagery slow you down. Think of the images that come to your mind as *weapons* you use to fend off demons or as *grievances* that are beginning to pile up.

- In the case of Tom, see his words here as invective hurled at the world for killing young people overseas in war and killing the heart and sanity of his elder sister in St. Louis.

- Obviously the entire speech cannot be a rant—but allow it to *become* a rant because your needs are so great. This creates the ability to play the opposites, ranting versus remembering, both of which are trying to break through you. Then you *earn* a pleasant reminiscence in the midst of the rant, in the same way you must earn a pause.

- The love of course is for his sister; let it also be for the dancing kids of Paradise Dance Hall as well, and the boys maimed and killed on the battlefield of Guernica, obliterated by those coming "bombardments." The love can also be a longing for his own misspent youth.

**Pitfall:** The speech becoming dreamy and wistful; being more about reminiscence rather than about an action; the actor losing himself in Williams' images.

**Solution:** Playing it as a fight against death and despair; as a call to arms; as an attack on the cost of war and insanity (his sister's). With speeches that appear to have a dreamy aspect, always choose *mire* (disruption, conflict) over *mood.* Lament the *loss* of the loving memory of the Paradise Dance Hall, and therefore the loss of the innocence you—and Laura and even Amanda—once had.

# 9. Choosing A Monologue

> Who chooseth me, shall gain what many men desire.
> Who chooseth me, shall get as much as he deserves.
> Who chooseth me, must give and hazard all he hath.
>
> *The Merchant of Venice*

When picking the monologue you want to use for audition I would like for you to make your choice based on these things:

### What Are You Auditioning For?

Who will be your audience? A theatre company or individual director? What sort of show(s) will he (they) do? Only realism? Only Shakespeare? Only musicals and light family fare?

### What Roles Are They Casting?

What are they casting? You must discover if they are casting a single show or a season of shows. It may be they will want to see more than one monologue but if they do not you will want to pick a speech that has enough movement and journeys of character so that they can see you go through a variety of beats and changes. I should say, however, that even if you are doing the auditions sponsored by SETC, Straw Hat or Unified Professional Theatre Auditions (UPTA) and are limited to one 60 second speech you will almost certainly need a few more at the ready to show the companies if they call you back. This is when they really want to see what you can do.

## What is Your Type?

Know and embrace your *type*. You must know and accept your type and make your monologue choice accordingly. This is one of the early hard but necessary lessons you will learn as an actor. Your type is as hard and fast as your DNA; even if you do what most people would suggest you do in order to change your type, even if you lose a lot of weight and change your hair color, it will still remain a rough climb to get people to think of you differently because it is not only about what you look like or are capable of doing it is about the *quality* you possess at first glance as a performer. Even if an actor is not tall (think of a host of Hollywood as well as Broadway leading men) they can come into a room and somehow *seem right* as a leading man; even if a young woman has a certain quirky way about her, even if she is not textbook 'beautiful' but rather 'striking' as people like to say, she can still read as *ingénue.* Because of what I brought to the table as an actor even as a fit, young man I still was never going to play Romeo. Type is what you are as you walk into the room without speaking, even after all the training and experience has made you the actor/actress you are today; you cannot change it and therefore you must embrace it with love or you are going to be in for a rough time trying to find work as an actor. If you are a portly character man you must not pick a speech from a young leading man or male character ingénue; if you are the scrawny female 'best friend' type you must not pick Juliet; if you would normally be thought of as Romeo then you must not pick a Friar Laurence; a Prince Hal type must not seek to do Falstaff. And there is an even more mercenary reason to pick your monologue based on type: you are not only picking to type because of casting, picking to type is, by definition, realizing that you must *exploit that which you do best as a performer.* If you are talented as a comic, have an affinity toward the dramatic or speak poetic language well Type is the fusion of what you look like plus what you do best and if you are careful—

—and not hard-headed; there are legions of chubby actors who stubbornly think they will do Hamlet some day! —You just might be able to 'type' your way into working all the time!

(By the way: the one reliable way to change your type is to *age*. As a matter of course a young actor plays old characters when they grow old and get fat. So it is that one day Juliet is destined to play the Nurse, Romeo to play the Friar. This is the surest way we have so far of 'changing' one's type.)

## What Do You Do *Best?*

Make sure the speech you have chosen will *sell* what you do best. Be it Lady Bracknell, The Artful Dodger, Blanche DuBois, Oscar Madison or thousands of other types. This is why you take the time to study what kind of plays the theatre will produce during their season; you are searching for the *roles* in those plays that you would play best. It is these kinds of speeches—those that *replicate* the part you want to be cast in— that you must choose in order to subliminally suggest to the director the part you want in his or her production.

## Are There Parts for You?

Does the director or theatre company have anything for you? This of course is related to type but it is more complicated than that. If they are doing a season of musicals and you do not sing or dance you might be out of luck. If they are doing Shakespeare and you are afraid of the language you are out of luck. If they are doing British drawing room comedies and you do not have a viable British dialect or sense of the style you are out of luck. (All of this said however I do encourage you to go ahead and do the audition anyway, even if you are not right. For one thing it is always a good idea to audition, even if it is ultimately just for the dreaded, 'experience.' And for another thing you never know; somehow, *somehow,* you just might manage to do something that catches their eye and causes them to take a chance on you. Even an unsuccessful audition is one single step closer to the audition that will win you the job.)

## Do What You can be Cast in *Now*

You must pick a monologue from a role you would be cast in right *now;* it may be that in a few years you will be able to play Willy Loman, but if you are Biff now you choose that. This includes range of skill, as well; it may be that one day your talent will be advanced to the point that you can do Hamlet; but for now—and this is the only arena in which you would play it safe— play it safe and do not take unnecessary risks. Choose the gravedigger (if you are a character man) or Horatio or Laertes (if you are a young type).

## Pick Monologues from *Plays*

Pick your monologue from *plays*. I am not a fan of this current vogue of looking to film or TV scripts for monologues for theatre; a theatrical monologue is structured differently than a film monologue. A film monologue has a different rise and fall, a different pay off, it is conceived with the notion that a camera lens will be literally inches from your face! A theatre monologue is built upon *size,* both physically as well as thematically, to accommodate the breadth and width of a sprawling thousand-seat auditorium with the knowledge that the viewer can be hundreds of feet away. Film and Theatre are different art forms, apples and oranges. We go to each for a different experience. Film requires you experience vicariously, *from a distance*, moved by what the actor is living that might have been shot months or even years before you observed it. As much as I am always moved at the end of *Casablanca* (and I am a film fan!) I know that this moment will forever be the same because it has been captured on celluloid for a hundred years to come. Film, then, wants you *passive*. Theatre on the other hand asks you to live each moment in *the here and now, alongside the actor as the both of you live and breathe*; no performance will ever be completely the same again. Theatre wants you *active*. This very nature sets up the scenario in which we are handed down stories and tales of legendary performances from the theatrical past; Laurette Taylor as the first Amanda Wingfield, Lee J. Cobb creating Willy Loman, Paul Robeson historical as Othello, Marlon Brando forever Stanley Kowalski. These long past performances and how they are remembered and spoken about is the very mythology of theatre: telling a story to someone outside of you and painting a picture of it so clear they can see it as clearly as you do! This is also the reason I would have you pick your monologue from plays; if you are to be a stage actor you ought to be well versed in dramatic literature, you should have an extensive working knowledge of the great plays, both contemporary as well as classics.

## Don't Pick Monologues from the Internet

I ask that you not pick your monologues from the hip Internet sites where young actors seem to want to go these days. Here is why:

1. Most of these Internet monologues do not have scripts; they are disembodied, concocted speeches meant to pass for genuine feeling or comedy without sufficient journey to produce that feeling or comedy.

2. In order to really work on your monologue you must be able to read the play from which it came to build the given circumstances; you must be able to know what came *before* your monologue, what made you speak it, the context of your speech, even though you will by definition be taking it *out* of context. You need that 'back story' even if you must change or adjust it to use the monologue for the audition.

3. The young actor seeking the stage must read plays, go to and read plays. This will not only feed your knowledge, but your *love* for theatre as well.

# 10. Working on a Monologue

Yet, by your gracious patience,
I will a round unvarnish'd tale deliver
Of my whole course of love; what drugs, what charms,
What conjuration and what mighty magic,
For such proceeding I am charged withal,
I won his daughter.

*Othello*


Work on your monologue this way:

1. Find in a play the speech spoken by a character of your type (or at least a character so neutral they can be played by an actor of any type).

2. As you do when working on a scene you must read the entire play, scanning it for reference to your character, especially scenes and moments that occur before the scene in which your monologue appears. Then bullet these moments for back story that can help motivate your monologue. Use every one of these scenes up to and including your monologue scene.

3. Memorize your monologue. You must know it backwards and forwards; this will afford you the freedom to experiment with it, applying various improvisations to it.

4. Do Stanislavski's work. This means asking these questions:
   A. Who are you talking to?
   B. What do you *want* from them or must *make* them *do?*
   C. What are you *doing* to get your objective?
   D. What obstacle(s) stand in your way?
   E. Are the obstacles a person or a force *outside of you?*
   F. Where is the *love* in the speech? If you cannot find it, find another speech.

5. Put together very simple staging. This can be done by constructing an imaginary circle all around you, stage center, about four or five feet on every side. Think of this as your "playing area." As you work on and perform your monologue try to remain in this circle. It will keep you from wandering too far L or R and help you stay fundamentally center. In any event if you find that you are wandering this means you are less clear on your objective and action and you need to clarify them.

6. I recommend not using a chair. 99% of the time there will be a chair available to you in the audition room, but I consider a chair a crutch. The only use I have ever seen chairs put to is when an actor for some reason or other has decided that a character wants to jump up out of it all of a sudden, as if to punctuate or react to something. Why not just react appropriately while already standing? Doing the other gives much more power to the chair than you want the chair to have; the scene, in effect, becomes *about the chair.*

7. Set your focus. This is very important. It is said—and I concur—that you must not perform your monologue to the people watching because you then place them in the unenviable position of 'playing the scene' with you. They do not want to do this; they want to be free and unbridled so that they can look at *you* and observe whether they think *you* are any good or not. Set your focus either just above their heads if you are in a room or at the EXIT sign at the back of the auditorium if you are in a theater. This will help

keep you pointed toward them without looking directly at them. This is particularly helpful with the soliloquy, in which your character is alone and hence fighting for something outside of them. So set your focus and do not stray from it; you look like an amateur when your field of vision waivers during the audition. Another good choice of focus when your speech has a specific person you are talking to is to place your 'partner' directly downstage to your immediate L or R. Make sure they are *downstage,* however; you must not place them to your far L or R side, this will commit the cardinal sin of presenting *profile* to the auditors.

8. See if any of the actions from the Outrageous List (found in Chapter 2) might be suitable for the actual performance of your monologue. Don't assume that, in an arena where you want to be deemed interesting in addition to talented, that all of your outrageous choices will be off limits.

I must say this: *more than half the time when I have given a student an "outrageous" adjustment to their monologue when they finally did it the action did not seem outrageous or out of place at all! In fact, in many cases it injected exciting new ways to look at the speech and even helped to make the speech more clear!*

After you have gotten comfortable with how your monologue plays, you might consider trying this:

a. At the time of the audition, come prepared with *two different versions* of your outrageous action, one more so than the other.

b. Try to gauge how the audition is going from the other actors around you, what you can learn about the theatre company or the director, if they seem willing to suffer your risk-taking. Your fellow actors are more than willing to share, "They were very nice!" with you as they come out of their audition. You always learn more about the audition when you actually get there than you had considered before.

127

c. When you get into the room you have only seconds to decide which of the two versions will be chosen. More than likely you will choose the one less outrageous; this is most often the correct choice. In any even I encourage you to *play*. You never know what might happen.

## Beginning, Middle and End

In your monologue you must present to the auditors a performance that has a beginning, middle and an end. In this regard you may truly look on your audition as a very short *play* in which you have taken them on a journey far away from their humdrum lives and then returned them safely back to their seats when you finally say, "Thank you."

### Beginning

Technically your monologue begins as soon as you enter the room. This is your *actor* portion of the speech; the *character* portion begins in the nanosecond that follows your introduction. At this point you must have built into your speech the need to speak.

I offer you these thoughts:

- Rehearse what your scene partner has *just* said that demands you reply. If it is from a specific scene in a play use that.

- If alone doing a soliloquy use the circumstance of the previous scene—or *make up* such a circumstance! It must be something that has *just* driven you into the room to *escape* the people outside so that you can find your answer in peace.

- Your first words are *demands to listen*. This is true if you are speaking to someone or if you are speaking aloud though alone. In the same way that in the midst of a heated argument you finally are forced to shout, "HOLD IT!" or "TIME OUT!" in order to get attention this is what the beginning of your monologue must be and do. Just remember that it need not necessarily be a shout you begin with, it must simply possess the kind of urgency a *desire to get attention demands.* As you work on your monologue you will discover what serves your speech best. The objective of the Beginning of your monologue should be, "I must get the attention of these people!"

## Middle

The middle of your monologue is where you truly fight for what you want. Give a care to this:

- After you have gotten their attention remember that during the middle of the speech you are *constantly making discoveries* that further support your premise and drive you to even greater and greater heights of discovery. Arguments go on and on because people remember *grievances* which caused them to speak up in the first place: the "AND *ANOTHER* THING!" moment. And because it is a *new* discovery this makes you rise higher and higher in pitch, need, energy, anger or joy. This helps your monologue "play" to the auditors.

## End

You have stated your case, fought and struggled, propelled by constant self-discovery along the way. Perhaps you are now exhausted; in any case you will probably be enervated by such strenuous human endeavor. Upon completing the journey you have just taken us on you will need to sum up all of what you have just said, *as if* you now say: "There you have it." Often such lines of this theme are already written into the well-written speech, such as Hamlet's final line of his most famous soliloquy:

Thus conscience does make cowards of us all,
And thus the native hue of resolution
Is sicklied o'er with the pale cast of thought,
And enterprises of great pitch and moment
With this regard their currents turn awry
And lose the name of Action.

Of course in the script here Hamlet discovers Ophelia and begins a scene with her. But you get the idea. You are done, and you are saying, "I am done," and your monologue must end. Try to find the spot where it appears most natural to stop, even if you need to edit the monologue to get there. I have done this many times when I was aware that a certain passage even if interrupted by another character's line, seems *right* as the place to end the speech. So you must end your monologue. This is piecing a monologue together, where you might find a scene written between two characters that has in it very nice single speeches spoken by one character but are interrupted by their scene partner. All you need to do is take out the lines you want and 'piece' them together.

When finished you then take a beat.

You say; "Thank you," and then you exit.

### Monologue for Practice:

### Mercutio
### The Queen Mab Speech

Here is a monologue to work on. This famous speech has been arguably the very reason –along with swordplay—to play the role of Mercutio in Shakespeare's *Romeo and Juliet*. Critics do not agree on what it means; they only accept that it is a very bear for an actor to assail. So try it out and put your stamp on it. And ladies, you try it, too; Mercutio has been played by women. First read the play, study the scene and all of the line notes at the bottom of the page, and then get busy. Where helpful do some of the iambic pentameter poetry stuff but don't let that bog you down. Shakespeare himself would be happiest if you just jump right in and *do it*. This speech was made to be outrageous with love. As you work on it, list possibilities for unexpected actions as well as making sense of the text. Answer all of the questions you must ask in order to do the speech. Just as there is a theme for a play, figure out what the theme might be for this speech. List all of the choices and try them all. Then pick the best one or two and do it!

MERCUTIO.

O, then, I see Queen Mab hath been with you.
She is the fairies' midwife, and she comes
In shape no bigger than an agate-stone
On the fore-finger of an alderman,
Drawn with a team of little atomies
Athwart men's noses as they lie asleep;
Her wagon-spokes made of long spiders' legs,
The cover of the wings of grasshoppers,
The traces of the smallest spider's web,
The collars of the moonshine's watery beams,
Her whip of cricket's bone, the lash of film,
Her Wagoner a small grey-coated gnat,
Not so big as a round little worm
Prick'd from the lazy finger of a maid;
Her chariot is an empty hazel-nut
Made by the joiner squirrel or old grub,
Time out o' mind the fairies' coachmakers.
And in this state she gallops night by night
Through lovers' brains, and then they dream of love;
O'er courtiers' knees, that dream on court'sies straight,
O'er lawyers' fingers, who straight dream on fees,
O'er ladies ' lips, who straight on kisses dream,
Which oft the angry Mab with blisters plagues,
Because their breaths with sweetmeats tainted are:
Sometime she gallops o'er a courtier's nose,

And then dreams he of smelling out a suit;
And sometime comes she with a tithe-pig's tail
Tickling a parson's nose as a' lies asleep,
Then dreams, he of another benefice:
Sometime she driveth o'er a soldier's neck,
And then dreams he of cutting foreign throats,
Of breaches, ambuscadoes, Spanish blades,
Of healths five-fathom deep; and then anon
Drums in his ear, at which he starts and wakes,
And being thus frighted swears a prayer or two
And sleeps *again.* This is that very Mab
That plats the manes of horses in the night,
And bakes the elflocks in foul sluttish hairs,
Which once untangled, much misfortune bodes:
This is the hag, when maids lie on their backs,
That presses them and learns them first to bear,
Making them women of good carriage:
This is she—!

What do I want?          Obstacles?
(You can experiment by listing more than one possibility)

1.                        1.
2.                        2.
3.                        3.

What do I *do* to get what I want?

Active Verbs                Outrageous Actions
1.                          1.
2.                          2.
3.                          3.
4.                          4.
5.                          5.
6.                          6.

# 11. Exercises for Monologues

Every night he comes
With musics of all sorts and songs composed
To her unworthiness: it nothing steads us
To chide him from our eaves; for he persists
As if his life lay on't.

*Alls Well That Ends Well*

In addition to actions from the "Outrageous List" I have provided here a few improvisations to help you energize your monologue. Naturally I hope they will be just what the doctor ordered but in the end the most important thing is that they get you moving, thinking, fighting ever more like a human being caught up in a situation they have never had to handle before. Each exercise can be used with either a classical or contemporary monologue.

## EVERY LINE IS A NEW DISCOVERY

This is a simple little improvisation that will help the actor remember how active and immediate their desire must be to fight for truth in a monologue. Try this:

- Stand and speak the speech out loud.

- Play the beginning of every new line as a *new discovery*, not thought of before.

- Play every new discovery as also a *surprise.* With every new line/discovery step in a completely different direction.

- As you draw near the end of the speech allow your voice to rise in pitch and your steps to take you off your feet, causing you to hop or jump or lunge.

- Stop. Now do the speech again, *immediately,* without the movement but keep the continuing discovery.


## ROOTING FOR 'GOLD.'

Get down on your hands and knees and begin your speech.

- Begin, like a dog, rooting on the floor as if you are digging with your bare hands.

- As you continue 'digging,' clamor from L to C to R and root harder, fiercer.

- The conceit is that you are feverishly digging for gold, or something *precious,* in the earth beneath you and that you are not able to find it. Allow your search to become more desperate, impatient, let it frustrate you to the point of being angry; where the devil *is* that thing I am looking for?

- As you go along allow your voice and reading of the monologue to be affected by your violent digging: pitch should build, words elongate, etc.

- Play it two different ways: one resulting in *finding* what you were looking for and another in which you *fail* to find it.

- Upon ending your monologue (and your search) let your celebration or your lament be on a long, wailing shout, not unlike the howl of a dog.

## *MAKE* THEM BELIEVE YOU!

As you begin your monologue throw in the following phrases; "Really!" "Honest!" "No, I'm not kidding!" "I'm NOT LYING!" "For REAL!" Do this constantly during the speech, after virtually every line, as if the made-up dialogue were part of the written monologue. Better yet, have either your teacher or a friend constantly interrupt you with negative words, such as, "I don't believe you! No, I don't! Stop lying! No way! Get out of here!" See how it drives the speech, how it almost causes you to overlap yourself, how it causes you to pick up your own cues without rushing because you are not artificially speeding up rather you are fighting to make yourself *understood and believed.* Then do the speech without the added words but continue to fight to be believed, to convince the audience that you are telling the *truth,* even and especially if it is in fact a bald-faced lie!

## *SHOUT,* THEN *WHISPER*

During the course of the speech, find a place, planned or unplanned, where you can SHOUT a line at the top of your voice. Just *one* line. Do the monologue several times this way. Then, do the speech again, *without* the shout, instead this time finding a spot where you can *whisper* a single line. In both cases it must be only a single line or, better yet, a single word. This can immediately energize the speech, giving emphasis, focus and drive. Sometimes it can even point up a deeper, more profound meaning in the monologue. I have done this exercise with actresses working on a speech of Little Bit from Paula Vogel's *How I Learned to Drive.* During the speech she is accusing Uncle Peck and at one moment during the monologue she mentions her age at the time he was molesting her. All the while I directed the actress to perform the speech as a casual, almost pleasant family reminiscence. However when she reached the word, "Twelve!" I suggested that she choose, then, to shout it at the top of her voice. *Twelve!* It was amazing what often would happen to the actress in the midst of the speech; she would get emotional, shaken, as if perhaps slapped in the face when faced with the realization of the deeper anguish, the horrific, true import of what Little Bit was confessing had been done to her.

After we blow up there is always the energy of *coming down* from having just blown up. This is what happens when we are forced to get control of ourselves; there is always a moment of being chastened, shamed and embarrassed at having let the cat out of the bag, of giving in to our greater vulnerability. So it is for the actor in the moment; in order to try to control yourself you must first *lose* control!

## *SING*, THEN *HA!*

In this exercise you find in your speech where you can simply take a single line—preferably with a period at the end of it—you can *sing out loud*. Obviously this is done all the time in musicals, we in the audience joy in the sudden song that warms our hearts and causes us to hum a tune. But not often do we do this as we pass through our day. You need not be a singer to do this, of course; people who sing out loud like this rarely are. Yet *something that happened within them at a certain moment caused them to feel the need to sing.* After the singing—and because it is, at least on the face of it, out of place and over the top and therefore impervious to ANY period or play or role—try to sense what doing it may have done to the speech, how it may have energized it. Has it punctuated the line that was sung? Has it added a new dimension to your thought of what your character wants in the scene? *Might* you be *actually* moved to sing a line as a jingle at a particularly inopportune moment? Might you? A fun variation on this exercise is for you to find a spot where you might interrupt yourself by shouting, "HA!" We cry when we should be happy, we laugh when we are sad and do we not, in a particular moment to celebrate a triumph, shout aloud, "HA"? And after the "HA!" see if it has unwittingly emphasized or punctuated the line or point before it, say, if Willy Loman were to blurt, "HA!" as a means to convince his son Biff that he is worthy of being great in life! Does not shouting "HA!" before a line tend to suggest braggadocio on the part of the one speaking? A sense of being wildly puffed up, confident, powerful, whether they are actually in such a position of power or not? Or, conversely, if the character is consciously deprecating themselves, putting themselves down, suddenly shouting, "HA!" can also suggest *giving up,* a certain pessimism about their prospects. (Just don't think in terms of the *retreating* kind of pessimism; make it rather an outgoing, grandiose, *narcissistic* pessimism. Never forget that, like all characters in a play, as shy and retiring as she appears even Laura Wingfield is an egomaniac!)


## HIT THE DECK!

This is a particularly risky exercise and one that I have only recently used to coach students. Up to now I have always felt that during the course of an audition, especially one for people who are going to presumably hire you, you wanted to avoid getting down on the ground. I always felt that there was just too much possibility of causing your movement to appear clumsy or uncertain, jerky or ungraceful at the end. Then I finally realized that if the actor has to sit or get down on all fours or otherwise get on the floor they should do so in the *middle* of the speech so that they can then more organically build a graceful rise to their feet by speech's end.

This exercise works best if you just *do* it during your speech, drop down to the floor just like that. Fall! Splat! Then continue speaking and see what happens. See how you might *rise up;* are you slow, fast, clumsy, graceful, confused or embarrassed while dusting yourself off? What does such a sudden violent act do to your monologue? your Objective? Action? Beats? Is it possible at all that such a thing could be worked *believably* into the body of the speech? Is it? Or does it stretch the 'Willing suspension of Disbelief' far too far for comfort? Just how outrageous is such an act? But of course how outrageous is the predicament your character finds him or herself in at that moment? Could you be so much at a loss that the only thing left for you to do at that moment is to throw yourself upon the mercy of...God? This can be the greatest benefit of such an improvisation; it can help the actor gauge just how outrageous, how life and death, how much *need* they are fighting for. Perhaps, unlike my concern for grace, the character is not concerned with graceful movement at all because they are so desperate to get what they want by the end of the speech? Suppose they genuinely want it that badly? Use your imagination; just *suppose*...

# 12. What I have Learned Watching Actors Audition

Nay, now you are too flat
And mar the concord with too harsh a descant:
There wanteth but a mean to fill your song.

*The Two Gentlemen of Verona*

O, she will sing the savageness out of a bear!

*Othello*

Here are a few thoughts I have had over many years of watching actors get up to 'strut their stuff.' I have also included notions that have occurred to me when auditioning actors for a play I am directing. Whenever I watch actors audition I always learn and my heart always goes out to them; I cannot say often enough that, truly, when you are up there we want more than anything in the world for you to be *good*. The only way we have to judge this, however, is by how much you have raised the stakes for your character and how hard and recklessly you have fought for your objective. In short, how *outrageous* you were!

# *Presenting Yourself*

### The First Second

In watching auditions over the years the one thing that stands out above everything else is the enormous importance of *the moment before you even begin your monologue.* During the audition whether I liked what I saw you do or not, whether I felt you were talented or not, after the fact I can never escape what almost always strikes me the very first second that I see you. Young actor, that incredibly short deceptively long second after you enter the room, just before you announce your name and number or the speech you will be doing are so unutterably important that it is unfair, but as an indicator of what I am about to see I have never seen it to fail. I urge you to be aware of this—for the auditors who sit in judgment of you certainly are—and to do all that you can to take hold of that precious moment every single time you audition. I urge you to rehearse every particle of what you do before you even enter the room: to go over your aspect with a fine tooth comb, to get coaching from an outside observer to pinpoint anything amiss about how you walk, gesture, or just plain "look," to rid yourself of even a *hint* that you could not want to be there. In this regard it is within your power to determine how we view you, what we think of you, maybe even if we decide to call you back to do more material—after all realize that a call back is not only because you are good, it is because the director just needs to see more of you to make their final decision.

### Up Good, Down Bad

In the midst of your scene or your audition the audience must never get the impression that you do not want to be there. In addition to acting and telling the story of the monologue you have chosen it must be obvious that you are right where you want to be, you would not want to be anywhere else in the world other than that audition room at that very moment—your desire to act and to be on the stage is that great. There are many ways that young actors betray themselves in this respect, and they do not always realize that they are doing it. One of the many ways that young actors fail at an audition—and this failure is very often before they have even begun their speech—is by habitually looking *down.* Because this is so important and because I have seen it so often I have come to call it, 'Up Good Down Bad.' This should be clear; when doing your monologue you must avoid looking down and on the other hand seek often to look up. It is that simple. When an actor is habitually looking downward during their monologue this tells me that somehow they are not comfortable with their surroundings or themselves or both; it means they are not clear on exactly what they are doing, where their focus must be, and therefore can do nothing better than look down, or downcast—and often they are not even aware of the fact that they are doing it! This, again, is related to training. I do not mean to say that the actor can never look down during a monologue—perhaps your character has just lost a contact lens and is desperate to find it, or, like Linda Loman during the Requiem in *Death of a Salesman* she is moved to look directly down at the grave of her husband Willy Loman—rather I am saying that the need to do so must be so great as to be obvious to your audience. Never forget you want their concentration on *you and your face* in order to appraise your acting ability. Why then would you do something that would cause even the auditors' gaze to be cast downward?

In coaching young actors I have found that for the most part this habit will go away as soon as the actor becomes clearer on *what they are fighting for in the speech,* what is their objective, and *exactly* how they are fighting for it—the active verb which will spark their action. Doing is the anchor the actor must cling to in the midst of the outrageously crazy and cruel circumstance of the play/audition; doing is the solace the actor must go to when trapped in that strange audition room, nervous out of fear of rejection. So go back and do your homework: *why are you speaking these words?* Why *must* you speak these words? To *whom* are you speaking? What do you want from them or what do you desire to make them do for you? What are you prepared to do to get these things? Where are you? Where have you come from?

Where are you going? And, admittedly a technical point but perhaps the most important one that I can mention regarding this subject: where is your *focus?* Where are you looking *specifically* while you are intentionally *not* looking at the audience (the directors) who are observing your audition? You must never look directly at them or play your monologue to them—they are not your scene partner; they are trying to decide if you are talented enough to hire and they cannot make this appraisal if you drag them into your scene! A very simple choice is to place your focus just *above their heads* if you are in a room or to the distant **exit** sign near the back if they are out in the theater auditorium. This is a technical, specific, easy thing you can do at once. Place your invisible scene 'partner' there and this will free the auditors to keep their eye on your face, body, movement and voice. It will also allow that special moment during the speech when the character must look down to be a *true* looking down rather than a nervous glance askance which betrays the fact that you do not want to be there and do not feel worthy. Erring in cheating your face UP helps them see your face, see you, your eyes, mouth, nose, and in so doing they will be seeing your character's needs and wants and desires, as well. You have so much farther to go if you go *up;* if a character in a speech is in a quandary look UP as the place where they can find an answer; UP is positive, is open, giving, freeing, revealing—and revealing the vocal chords, too! *Down* on the other hand is retiring, is faltering, fading, shying away, trying to hide or perhaps worst of all not knowing what to do and therefore choosing nothing, trying instead to sink into the floor. If you make a mistake, make it in terms of giving (UP) rather than taking away (DOWN).

### Don't Hide from Us

In the midst of your audition you must never let the auditor get the impression that you are hiding from him or her. This is different from Up Good Down Bad, which I just spoke about. By hiding I mean you must stage your speeches so that you can be seen clearly—don't set up the imaginary person you are speaking to immediately to your left or right; this will cause you to present only profile. I also mean by hiding that you must make choices which *liberate* you rather than *chain you down.* You must fight for something that is up and *outside* of the character, something that is *past* the footlights. If you err in making movement choices based on need let the error be that you are looking up too much; at least this will help the auditors see you better. What your character is fighting for must be so earth-shattering they are about to lunge from the stage after it; don't let anybody get the idea that you are more comfortable being far up there on the stage, in order to be *"away from us."*

One last form of hiding is by making choices that are safe and mundane rather than outrageous and challenging. Plays are not safe! Plays are not about hiding! *They are about hidden things that come to light!*

### Your Audition Begins as You are *about* to Open the Door

Your audition begins as you are about to open the door because that is the point of no return. It is every bit as the first moment you step upon the stage, you are *out there,* and you must be focused and ready, completely free of any confusion or distractions. Any requirement of bathroom or first line attack or moment to blow up or calm down or sum up your monologue has been rehearsed and "conned by rote" and you are therefore able to be free to be "yourself." When your hand grasps the door knob or when the stage manager opens the door beckoning you to come in, if you had to you would be ready *then* to spout the first words of your speech without any time required to "get into it." In that regard your audition begins as you are about to open the door, so be prepared.

### Your Entrance is Your *First* Bit of Blocking

Your entrance is part of your staging. Your *first* bit of staging. Rehearse your entrance just as you would your whole monologue package, complete with the *genuine* smile you will have on your face as you enter. The auditors must get the impression that you are, in addition to being tremendously talented, *delighted* to be there.

## Your Introduction Proves How Professional You Are

How should you introduce your monologue? Never ever say, "I will be performing a scene…" or "This is the scene where…" Personally I even have a problem with saying the word, 'piece,' or 'monologue.' With all due respect it makes me think of community theater. It is not necessary to say, "monologue"; they know it's a monologue. I would suggest you Introduce your audition this way:

> *"Hello. My name is John/Jane Doe. This is (Character Name) from (Title of the Play)."*

Short and sweet.

Or if you are doing a speech of one of the great roles, such as Hamlet, Othello, Macbeth, Blanche Dubois, etc., you can simply give the character name. (They will know the play; trust me!)

In announcing your monologue you are doing much more than telling the auditors what you will be performing. You are telling them that you are a professional who wants to be there, who is happy to be there; who is so glad to be there that you almost can't contain yourself. You are telling them that you are not only talented and right for the part for which you are auditioning, you are also saying that you are a good clean kid who will not cause any problems for the director during the show; that you will be on time and prepared and imaginative and fearless and easy to get along with and will take direction well. You will be saying all this and more; in those few seconds they (meaning the auditors) can tell as soon as you enter the room whether you want to be there, and whether or not they believe you are any good, as soon as you open your mouth. Yes; they know this right away. Watch a few hours of unified auditions sometime and you will discover this yourself. That is why it is *wise to rehearse your introduction even as much as you rehearse your speech!*

## Getting 'Into It' Before You Start

If you have had the chance to witness mass auditions such as are conducted across the country perhaps you have seen this; the actor enters, announces their name/number or the speech they are doing, and then they proceed to bow their head or turn their back with bowed head for a beat of one, two …and *then* turn back or look up to launch into their audition! Should you take a moment to 'get into it'? No. You should have done all that preparation on the other side of the door before you came in. Spare your auditor the out of date, stagey "I'll turn my back now and then turn around and *wow* them!" Be ready to explode into your speech even as you are announcing your name and the monologue you will be doing. Be prepared to 'wow' them as soon as you make your entrance. When you do the 'turn around' it sets up the expectation that whatever happens when you finally do turn back is going to be wonderful— so it had *better* be! Avoid this. It says that you were not "ready" when you came in.  Such a block-buster after a turned back and bowed head rarely happens; if you were good enough to produce that kind of a reaction after doing this good for you but I have never seen it happen in 30+years, and I would add that if you were that good you are good enough to do it without the turnaround. Warm yourself up properly and completely as you wait *outside* the door so that when your name is called to go in you are, in effect, *already* doing your monologue as you smilingly enter the room! This is what I am talking about when I speak of knowing exactly when your monologue begins. The nervous energy you will certainly have while waiting for your time to audition can be channeled into the beginning of your speech. Then you just might 'wow' them.

## Using a Chair is a Crutch

Do not use a chair; stand and move. Let the appearance/staging of the monologue be about *you*. If you feel you must have a chair, stage it also without. 99.9% of the time there will be a chair in the room for your use, but just the same you don't want to be thrown by that 1% when there isn't one. And think about what I just suggested: if a chair is so germane to a speech that you are forced to rehearse it two different ways isn't that too much trouble over an object which is, after all, just an object?

## How to Move When You *Must* Move

Don't move too much, especially 'just to move.' (Even though you will be doing it 'just to move.') Allow only minimal blocking to happen, and it must be allowed to come organically out of your needs in the speech; that is, what your character is fighting for. Give careful consideration as to whether you will get down on the floor. I have evolved on this notion, where once I did not advise an actor to do it during an audition. If you do, remember that you will have to *get back up,* and you want this to be as graceful and clean as possible; build it into the action/needs of the monologue. Better yet, if you get down onto the floor choose to do it during the middle of the monologue so that you have the rest of the scene to get back to your feet. The only real rule here is that whatever you choose to do in moving, the person who sees you do it must be allowed to at least *possibly* believe that it happened because of the outrageous situation your character found themselves in—or, if not believable, so risky and outlandish and daring that you must be given credit for being fearless. By your audacious talent and imagination you may force the auditor to think, 'Bravo!' After all, in entering the audition room in the first place you already have taken the greatest risk imaginable; you might as well go the rest of the way.

## Miming Makes you Look like an Amateur

If your audition monologue requires the use of props and you do not have them it is best not to attempt to mime them. Even if you were the most stunning mime in the world you would not serve yourself in miming objects. The speech must be about *you and your needs,* not about demonstrating how well you can imagine objects that are not there. There is even the danger that you might give the auditor the impression that you were better to perform on the streets of Central Park than in their theatre company. Never mime anything that the character must actually have; then the speech is about how well (or how poorly) you mime. If you must mime, use only the kind of *gestures* a person speaking would when describing something they *know they do not have in their hands,* such as pointing, indicating or talking on a telephone. This way we know that you know that you do not have the object and you are clearly not attempting to visually *create* anything other than what your need is in speaking. That said a speech that requires that much mime probably should not be used at all. You are not auditioning for a mime troupe; you are trying to 'hold the mirror up to nature' using the entire canon of dramatic literature!

## Props Make You Look like an Amateur

Should you use props at your audition? Nine out of ten times, I would say No. In addition to looking amateurish and desperate props give the impression that you have no imagination, that you actually need to have what you are talking about, rather than being able to paint the picture of those things through your acting. Many years ago when Actor's Equity still required the old Equity Principal Interviews, I attended one for Delaware Theatre Company. In line behind me that day was a young lady who asked me to let her know when I thought we might be called into the room to interview and hand over our pictures and resume (the room was set up to accommodate two actors at once). I told her I would and gave her the 'hi' sign when I thought our time drew near. I turned back to face the door and eventually my time to go in came. The young actress behind me appeared suddenly into the room, approaching the other gentlemen seated next to the man I was about to meet. She had dashed off to the ladies' room and put on a full *French maid's costume, complete with feather duster*! She clearly had mistaken the call and was hoping to do a monologue of Doreen from Moliere's *Tartuffe!* All she succeeded in doing, however, was shock the poor guy sitting across from her. All that effort, a full costume, for what? (I do not know if she was ever offered the chance to audition later but I can tell you from the wide-eyed look on the face of the Artistic Director, I think not!)

Those precious moments you are on stage in the audition room must be selfishly, ravenously devoted only to *you,* not to a prop not to a costume. We want to see who you are and glimpse the depth of your talent, confidence and imagination. If there is any prop which is as important as that, don't be surprised if the auditor chooses to hire the prop instead.

That said, I did indicate that *nine* out of ten times do not use a prop. It is possible that there can be *one* call back situation so rare as to help you if you are auditioning for something specific and are then able to indicate a targeted, clear point of reference related to your character and the prop. A theatrical agent buddy of mine tells me about an audition he observed for *Evil Dead The Musical* in which the actress had chosen to plant many tiny, fake plastic spiders all over her person, which at the appointed moment during her song she plucked out, to amusing winning effect. So use of a prop can be useful in the right circumstance—I would suggest the *call back,* because the auditors have already seen you and liked you and want to see more of you in context of the play.

More Points to remember about presenting yourself:

- Don't place the 'person you are talking to' in a chair. *Then the speech is about how well you can talk to a chair.* Again, let the speech be about *you* and how *you* react to what your imaginary partner is saying. Place them in the position of *standing in front of you.* Do this even if in context they *would* be sitting.

- Don't place the imaginary person to whom you are speaking at your profile Left or Right; put them out front, downstage of you. Your focus should be out front and no farther L or R than just off C. You want the auditors to be able to see your face at every moment.

- Don't show them Profile. As your need drives your movement and focus in the speech you will undoubtedly be looking from left to right, but the auditor wants to see your *face,* full front, at least as much as possible.

# *When I Am Casting a Play*

When I myself am casting a play naturally I observe but my thoughts and impressions are focused much more on the particular show I am directing, less generally abstract. Here are some of my secret thoughts, just for you:

## Dress

- You can guess that this a pet peeve of mine by how often I have chosen to mention it. I am not thrilled to see someone dressed in jeans with holes in them, frayed cuffs flopping on dirty sneakers, wrinkled T-shirts. It makes me feel that the person auditioning for me does not care much about me or the play they are auditioning for. Of course I give people slack about this if they are college students, but you have to learn *some* time, do you not?

- I really appreciate clean, neat dress. No need to be formal as much as presentable. Think corporate casual.

- My ideas change if I am casting *Orphans* and want to see the actors grungy. But then I would have stated that in the casting notice beforehand, wouldn't I?

- The above said, I have never refused a good actor because I might not have liked their dress; I may have pet peeves but I am not an idiot!

- Women: heels, but not too high (character shoes work best); hair combed and back of your face; light make-up; a skirt preferably—not too short— but dark slacks are okay as well. No wild colors or garish jewelry.

149

- Men: ironed shirt, slacks. I do not require a sport jacket or tie but it is acceptable. I will allow jeans if they look clean or new. Hair neat and combed. I am not thrilled to see a pony tail but keep it tied back and away from your face. Beard either well trimmed or clean shaven. (I once saw a young man get up to audition whose beard and hair were so long in league together he looked like Rasputin. If that was the role I was casting, he was in. Otherwise not so much!)

- The above said is also because of Type. I must risk being thought politically incorrect here: auditors want to see Men who look like Men and Women who look like Women.

### Beginning

- Listen to me very carefully: the first words you speak in your monologue or reading from the script is VERY important, maybe the most important. Many of my impressions, for good or ill, are made at this moment.

- I like a big, clear voice. (This suggests confidence.)

- I appreciate action: that is, *doing something right away.* This suggests—fairly or not—talent as well as self confidence.

- The number one thing I hear from directors and theater professionals about student actors' auditions is *THE STAKES ARE NOT RAISED HIGH ENOUGH.*

- I appreciate levels: being big, then small, then big again, etc. I like being taken on a journey.

- I am BORED by a monologue that is only on one level. That is, if you seem to be the SAME at the *end* as you were at the beginning.

- I suggest OVERDOING rather than UNDERDOING. If I am compelled to ask you to do it again and tone it down, I will. But I will appreciate the fearlessness. As long as it does not appear desperate.

- SUBTLETY is overrated as far as I am concerned. Almost *never* is an actor as big—or as *Over the Top*—as they think! I personally have never seen a young actor at an audition go over the top.

- It helps to *smile*. Really, it does!

## Adjustment

- I will often give you a note after a reading or audition monologue. I am trying to see if you can take direction and *go further, drawing from your own imagination,* with what I have suggested. I will love you if you take a suggestion I have given you and make it something big and different.

- Sometimes I give you a note just to reassure myself I have given you a second chance.

- Often I will give you a note just to see if you can be bigger. If it is not then big enough I may even repeat this, giving you another chance, but I am disappointed when I have to give you the note more than once; this causes me to feel then and there that I cannot use you in my show. Not because you are not trying, but because it appears to me that you cannot be big enough for the stage.

- Most of the time, if I LOVE your work I will dismiss you *almost right away.* This is why actors should never assume anything from how an auditor appears to treat them. *I dismiss you so quickly because I know that I will be calling you back—I know that I am interested in you!* I do this because I want to get on to the next person who is waiting;

there may be a lot of people out there in the lobby. I know I will be seeing you again at Call Backs.

## Reading

- When reading from the script hold it up to your eye level, not down at your chest or waist as most people do. This will keep your focus up. You will be able to see your scene partner just over the top of your paper.

- I recommend highlighting in YELLOW your lines if you have sides that you were able to work on beforehand.

- When in doubt be LOUD and BIG.

- *Play* with your partner, look them in the eyes, touch them, do all that you can with them while still holding a script.

- You are *still reacting* while your scene partner is reading; don't drop out of the scene.

- If you make a choice *go all the way.* Being tentative will hurt you in my eyes; I will think that you will hold back from me as well as your fellow actor. If you are wooing someone, be all over them; if you are arguing with someone, get in their face. They are actors, too; probably they will give you back just what you gave them and we will then have a lot of fun.

- You will win no rewards for trying to make the *right* choice; what is right can only be discovered working with the director in rehearsal after you have been cast. You must concentrate on *making* a choice, and a *big* one. Fail BIG rather than fail small!

- As long as no one gets hurt and you do not take off your clothes and your partner is comfortable with what you are doing you are free to do almost *ANYTHING*. You have my permission.

### More Thoughts

- Again—this cannot be said enough—you are making an impression before you even open your mouth!

- Do the audition for YOURSELF, not for ME. Do not attempt to please me or do what you *think* I would want you to do. Do what *you* like and believe is right for the monologue!

- I really appreciate a surprise!

- I will stop you once I have learned *all that I need to know*. Please don't take it personally if I do not allow you to finish your monologue or if you read the scene only once or half way through.

- I really want you to be good when you come in.

- I really appreciate your guts to even get up there.

- Keep auditioning even if you are not cast at first.

---

## *Acting Your Monologue*

### Where Have You Been?

Literally, the given circumstances of the play are probably 'where have you come from?' But for the dramatic needs of the speech it is helpful and more interesting to make it 'what has *propelled* you into this room?' What has *driven* you to speak what you are now speaking, experiencing before our very eyes?

## Outside of You

A monologue is about something *outside* of you which you are forced to fight for. In the speaking of it aloud you are not talking to yourself; rather you are moved to speak out loud to *whoever* may hear with the hope that they will come and rescue you!

## For Comedy don't try to be Funny— Just Be a *Human Being!*

You must never try to be funny with a comedic speech (you should not do this even if you *are* funny!). You must portray a human being caught up in an outrageous situation caused by love. Though the comic monologue must be funny, consider the rich possibility of a speech in which at least a *little* pathos might be injected. Once again: *antithesis.* In either speech you want the sense of them to be clear but you are shown to best advantage if you can also display complexity as well. For Comedy think strong choices that clash with the strong choices made by your scene partner. That is, *conflict.*

## Dramatic is Not Being Angry and Crying All the Time!

Your dramatic speech must be serious, perhaps even sad, must have fire and brimstone and maybe once or twice even require that you explode, but just the same you must not be yelling at the auditor to the top of your voice for the whole time. Quite the opposite; this is what it means to employ the concept of "Less is more." Less is More does not mean that you mumble and whisper; it means that the mumbling and whispering *comes out of the fact that you either just did or may well blow up at any moment.* Your character is fighting for their life in an outrageous situation beyond their control; out of frustration one is going to lose it and then have to tamp it down and lose it and have to tamp it down again. Therefore your character should be…*human.*

## Positive Choice

This is one of the most important acting notes; making a *positive* choice. This does not mean that you are happy or a good guy or being agreeable. It means positive in the sense of *moving the action forward and needing the other person in the scene.* Plays and drama are about people who MUST communicate, who MUST talk, who MUST fight, love, seek the truth. Even—and especially—when your character says, "I don't want to talk to you. Leave me alone!" What they actually mean is that we MUST talk and settle this thing right here and now! The only time you may believe that a character truly does not wish to talk to another character, when they truly wish to be left alone, is if the playwright has written that they then *exit the room!*

Think of what seems to be coldness from one character to another as that character fighting to *send a message* to the person they are being cold to! Their coldness is a *tactic* through which they will gain the chance to confront the other, to set the stage for the argument, lay the groundwork for the coming *inevitable* fight with this person!

## Negative Choice

Avoid making a negative choice, either with the introduction of your speech or the performance of it. This is related to hiding but is more damaging to your audition. It is causing the auditor to feel that you don't really want to be there, what you are about to do is not really that good, and maybe you had better be on your way. Most often it comes in the form of body language; uncertainly stepping into the room, habitually looking down—Up Good Down Bad which I mention above—losing energy at the end of a line, not fully hitting the consonants, elbows that appear to be locked into your sides, avoiding eye contact with the auditor even upon coming into the room. This is another reason that it can be advantageous to rehearse your entrance and the introduction of your monologue; this bit of stage "business" will help to anchor you as you nervously come into the room. Come in smiling like a human being happy to be there—*truly* happy to be there, and not a tense, horrific pasted-on toothy smile, either—and proudly (projecting just the right amount of pride) proclaim your name and what your monologue(s) will be. Then perform the speech and say a genuine "Thank you" and get out.

## Rushing

You will not want to give the impression that you are rushing. This can be an unfortunate bi-product of the 60-second mass cattle call audition; causing the actor to "go fast" merely because they have a limited time to get through their speech. Even if a director gives you a note to 'pick up the pace'—that is, to *go* fast—they are not actually asking for this. What they are asking for—and what you want to fight for in your audition monologue—is a driving, immediate, visceral *need* which propels you forward because you *are so desperate you cannot wait to win your objective.* This will keep the scene moving and cause you to *appear* to be going "faster." Best of all it will lead you to greater clarity in the playing of your objective.

## Energy at the End of a Line

You must also keep up the energy at the end of the speech, when your character is forced (either because of being interrupted or they must fight for better words to say) to pause or stop. They are not done; rather they are struggling to find *even better* words to express what is burning inside them trying to burst out. This is especially true of the Shakespearean rhymed couplet at the end of a scene. Rhymed couplets in Shakespeare must be pointed up and focused outward, proclaiming to the audience that 1: The scene is over but either way 2: There is a lot more to come!

## Explode Part Two

I repeat myself here, with a few more thoughts. With your audition you want to display your innate fire and yes, danger. So a carefully—and *strategically*—chosen explosion in your speech is good and dramatically, dynamically necessary. You simply cannot blow up all the time; otherwise it will be meaningless. Once you are aware that an explosion is called for in a scene/speech, look also for the moment when the character is *striving to calm down.* You are also doing this because you want to leave them wanting to see more. Always leave them wanting more; wanting to find out how it all ends, what happens next, how your character makes out, etc. If you give them more there is always the danger they will not like what you give them. These thoughts might be helpful:

1.  Explode only *once.* Save it for the right moment. (But I do not mean the 'pay off' type speech!)

2.  Play and take ample time for the 'calming down' *after* the explosion. Be aware of what happens to you after you have just blown up. There are a lot of potential acting values here, think of yourself in real life: if you have just yelled at someone are you not energized? Is your heart not beating rapidly? Do you not require a moment—perhaps even longer than that—to calm down? How we react after a great show of emotion can be more interesting than the out-pouring of that emotion in the first place. Think of the 'calm down' as Part Two of your explosion. Even if we are yelling at someone we do not like (versus shouting out of frustration linked to love) we are not happy with ourselves after, not happy with our *failure;* in those seconds after the blow we go through a lot things, think a lot of things, *feel* a lot things, before we are moved to finally reply, "I'm sorry I yelled…" As an actor be aware with fine-tuned precision what is happening to you in the moment—and also what is happening to your scene partner.

3.  The explosion may be vocal, but remember that it is the pent-up frustration *inside you* which has boiled over, and there are many ways both physical as well as vocal to display this. How about a SILENT explosion? How about one great unintelligible burst of sound without words before you continue on with your speech?

## Lose it for Good Stuff as well as Bad Stuff

I spoke about "Seeming to Lose Control" in Chapter 7. This is geared for the audition and it is different from the occasional, impulsive **explosion**. During your monologue you must come at least close to losing it. What does this mean?  Wailing and screaming and crying?  Of course not. There are two things I want to say about the monologue version of "losing it." First: *It means that such an event is certain to happen if you keep going on.* The possibility of losing it must simmer underneath the very beginning of your speech and it threads throughout the entire sixty seconds or two minutes you are speaking; you are a human being thrown into an outrageous, hopeless loving situation and you are doing your *best* to fight your way out of it, but there is always that danger that you just might not be able to hold on and so you—lose it. Second: Losing It *can be for good as well as bad.* A nice comedic moment is possible when a character seems to be on the brink of going hysterical with *happiness;* think of Malvolio in the garden with the letter in *Twelfth Night:* we are joyously happy for this stiff Puritan as well as amused by his excitement when he thinks Olivia is in love with him! Whether you lose it or not depends upon the speech you are doing. It may be that you will not want or need to lose it; there only needs to be the *possibility* of it happening, which just might cause the auditor to want to see more as you leave the room.

## *Go* Somewhere and Take *Us* with You

Your monologue should take us—and you—somewhere. Even though it is only two minutes or less, we in the audience want to feel as though we have gone on a long journey with you. Your performance must ideally have a beginning, middle, and end, all of which must be gotten into and out of cleanly. Going somewhere, taking the character through something, helps you be different at the end from the way you were at the beginning. You must always, somehow, *change.*

## How long should your Monologue Run?

Times have changed. It used to be that you were given 5 minutes to do two monologues. Now 2 minutes seems like forever. Nowadays I think 90 seconds is best; this will allow for an internal 'change' or 'journey' without feeling rushed. In any event you should stop your speech sooner than you might think. Beware of 'saving that big moment,' that big payoff; if you must have a payoff *start* with that and work your way forward far enough to fashion a speech that is 1 minute and 30 seconds in length. For the 60 second 'Cattle Call' unified auditions 45-55 seconds is *plenty* of time. You will still however have to make sure you have normal length monologues handy for your call back.

## *Ending* your Audition Shows You are Professional Too

It is a logical notion, in the heart of the anxious actor who has worked hard and honestly wants to please the director and get the job, to wonder if you should wait for any notes the director may want to impart to you at the end. Should you wait for this?   Never. Once the audition is over say "Thank you" and leave the room at once, like a professional. If they want you they will say so then or phone you soon thereafter. Do not hesitate as if you thought they were going to call you back then and there and offer you a contract. (Sometimes they will call you back right away. This is a good thing, of course, but don't wait for it to happen. They might realize just how desperate you are to get the part.)

Never linger as if to *allow them the time* to say, "What is your availability?" If they are interested, believe me, they WILL ask you this. Also, NEVER ask an agent or director or producer why you did or didn't get a part. Even if you do get the part, not always will it be the reason you wanted to hear. (Think, "You were the right height or "the right hair color" to match up with the person I REALLY wanted who has already been cast.

# *Monologue Choice*

The list of do's and don'ts are legion these days. Let me speak in general terms about your choices. Depending upon your audition, it may be that you will only be able to do one 60 second speech. If so a good choice in such short order is comedic, and if you can only do one the best first choice would be from a play by Neil Simon (although you do want to avoid the "Mr. Cornell" speech from *Star-Spangled Girl.* [10]). Christopher Durang can be a possibility but proceed with caution as some of his more acerbic sketches have been added to many "Overdone Monologue" lists (such as the "Tuna Sandwich" speech[11] and the "Tinker Bell is Dead" speech[12]); your comedic character must, above all else, be *likeable and honestly fighting for something.* If you choose a dramatic monologue you have an unlimited storehouse but remember here that it cannot be simply about yelling at the auditors the entire time (a potential pitfall for my Joe Mott speech); you want a speech which has levels, takes your character—and us—through a journey so that you are different at the end than you were at the beginning. Below are a few thoughts about monologues to choose and avoid.

## Your Monologue Must Be a Role You Could Play Now

Choose your monologue from a role in a play you would be cast in right now. If you are in your 20's don't pick a speech from a character who is in their forties; if you are a fat character actor don't choose a slim romantic lead; if you are a young woman don't pick an old dowager. If (and it HAS been done, I've seen it!) you are white don't choose a Black character from an August Wilson play. No one must be more hard core and cruelly realistic about Type than you, because you want to be cast, you want to work. A monologue speech must never be from a role you hope to play *some day.*

---

[10] Neil Simon, "The Star-Spangled Girl," 1967, Dramatists Play Service.
[11] Christopher Durang, "Laughing Wild," 1987, Samuel French, Inc.
[12] Christopher Durang, "Dentity Crisis," 1978, Samuel French, Inc.

## The "Pay Off at the End" Monologue

You must never choose a speech for a perceived great moment at the end that is going to 'wow' them. Doing so always makes the actor do conspicuously less *during* the speech—because they are intending to "save themselves' for the big blowout at the end! If such a moment is coming, why make us wait? Those of us who are watching have already decided what we think about you; to make us wait for your 'great moment' will be too late. Do this: pick a speech that has a whammo pay-off at the end and then *start* the speech with that same wham and go *farther* when it finally comes!

## Don't Do the 'Memory' Monologue

Don't do a monologue about remembering something unless you can apply it to what you are fighting for in the *here and now*. Actors love to do a speech on stage where the character is looking back; they can get dreamy and wistful, they get to show the audience that they can be "real" on stage. What they don't realize however is they are attempting to film act, *on stage*. A stage play cannot pan up close to your face like a camera, gentle mood music playing to punctuate your gentle words—if it could it would cease to be *theatrical!* A piece about a mood ceases to be about a human being fighting for something in an outrageous situation because it is inherently *inactive*. A monologue with a similar danger of this which I spoke of earlier is Tom's "Paradise Dance Hall" speech from *The Glass Menagerie*. My same suggestions would apply if you feel that you just must do a speech built on reminiscence:

- It must be about fighting your way through to a truth in the moment *here and now*.

- You must not give in to the urge to *listen to your own voice*.

- The speech must be a fight to *regain* those happy days!

- Or the speech must a fight to *overcome the scars you suffered* so long ago!

This type of speech is also by its nature very indulgent; in the same way the audience does not need you to help them along with feelings or prompt them to like you they also do not need you to demonstrate how lovely or horrible your character's past was. Don't play mood—fight for an Objective! Uta Hagen said, quoting an acting teacher of hers, "Mood spelled backwards is *Doom!*"

### A Phone Call Speech is Not a Monologue!

Phone Call Monologues only beg the question of 'who are you talking to?' without presenting you as a human being fighting for something in an outrageous situation. The very nature of the phone call means the person you are speaking to is not with you in the room; if your imaginary scene partner is there you can react to them in the moment, on time, right here and now; if the person is on the other end of the line you cannot fully relate to them because you cannot reach out and touch them. They also present the 'mime' problem an actor must always avoid; creating an object you do not have which your character must have. Already the speech has become not about you and your needs but about how well—or poorly!—you are creating an invisible telephone! Then the speech is about the phone, not about you! Hang up on the phone call monologue!

### The 'Feel Sorry for Yourself' Monologue

Emotion is the actor's stock in trade, but be careful of too much of it. Present a person who is doing the best they can and then we will be with you better if you just get to the *precipice* of tears, not the gushing out of them. Acting is not therapy; if you want to bawl on somebody's couch there are professionals you can go to. There are speeches in which the character betrays deep and profound vulnerability and it may well be that tears would be a believable eventuality. But your character's emotion is about much more than what they are showing in the moment; it is also about their fight for their heart's desire yet to be concluded, in which we in the audience are meant to see some great truth about *our own lives*. So always think about fighting against the torrent of tears that want to come; they just may come as a result of this, of course, but we will be galvanized along the way by your brave face.

## The 'I am So Awful Speech'

Don't do the "I am so awful" speech. Alma from *Summer and Smoke,* handled poorly, comes to mind as a danger. Also, in a different way, is the Jennie "I'm worth it!" speech from Neil Simon's *Chapter Two* (And actually this speech is also on the dreaded, "Overdone Monologue" list). These speeches are very much akin to the Feel Sorry for Yourself speech, both of which can be a kind of perverse egoism (O poor ME!). Your character must be neither saint nor sinner, Little Red Riding Hood nor the Big Bad Wolf. They simply must be doing the best they can even if they fail. I have heard it said that psychologically, perhaps subliminally, directors and producers sometimes get the notion *you* are the screw up raved about in your speech. If you find that you must do a speech that has an 'I am so awful' quality try to find the beat during the speech where the character can rise to the occasion and really *fight to overcome their predicament.* Then you will be creating variety and more levels and you will be showing them, yes, *range.*

## The Dirty Word Monologue is a Crutch

Unless you are auditioning for a show which contains it or are otherwise requested to provide it, you are best to avoid scatological language in a monologue. True, you are auditioning for people who probably use such language constantly in private, but in the audition room you are not aware of the sensibilities of the auditors (in the large unified auditions for example) and it is best not to offend. But, perhaps more importantly, such language can become a gimmick in which you curse and swear merely for *effect,* as if to feign the danger and edginess you should have had to begin with. Strive to shock the auditors with your intensity as a human being, not by your potty mouth. It may well be that one day you will be called upon to do the "F-----g Ruthie!" speech from Mamet's *American Buffalo.* But in the initial audition—unless told otherwise—you want to present to the auditor someone who is *talented* enough to be *any*one, *any*where, *any* time!

### Don't Do Monologues from Movies

As I said in Chapter 9 I would prefer that you didn't; not for a stage audition. If you are auditioning for the stage you must choose a speech from a play, written for the stage and therefore constructed to be theatrical in size and desire. There are plenty of theatrical speeches which will allow you to be intimate and small, in terms of the *stage.* You do not need to canvas screen plays to find them.

### Don't *Experiment* During Your Monologue

Don't experiment with a monologue at the audition. Do not seek to 'challenge' yourself at an audition. The biggest challenge of all is that you are there in the first place; in getting up to audition for complete strangers you are trying to stack the deck in your favor. This means minimizing your faults and maximizing your good points. Even when you are doing two speeches, classical and contemporary/dramatic and comedic you are still choosing only material that you can hit out of the park! 'Showing your range' means that you are showing them the great range you possess *now,* not that range you hope one day to broaden.

## Classical Monologues

### When they Ask for 'Classical' they Mean Shakespeare!

A theatre company wants to hear how you handle the greatest dramatic literature of all time, and therefore they mean, when they ask for a classical monologue, the works of William Shakespeare. Look closely at the casting notices; if they want Moliere couplets or Greek verse they will say so. They want to hear how you "handle" blank verse, otherwise known as the infamous Iambic Pentameter. They want to hear if you can speak it in such a way that makes it both accessible and classic. If it is comedic and in prose (as most of Shakespeare's comedic characters speak) they want to be assured that you are able to make sense of the 400 year-old slang. In other words they want to hear you speak it like it was your everyday speech, and at the same time move their heart or tickle their funny bone. Certainly there will be the occasional Goldsmith, or Marlowe, or Beaumont & Fletcher speech; but why not seek first from the very best?

## Doing a Shakespeare Monologue

Please consider these few thoughts when doing a Shakespeare monologue:

1. Do the Stanislavski homework. What are your Objective, Action, and Obstacle?

2. Practice the Laban 8 efforts. They are an excellent tool to incite physical expression in words, which is what the work of the Bard requires.

3. There is very little subtext in Shakespeare. His characters say what they mean and mean what they say...in great detail!

4. Make a discovery, a *new* discovery, with *every line you say*. Your character did not plan to say what they say; they have just discovered it in the moment! (And by the way: this is good advice for contemporary monologues as well!)

5. Play the *antithesis*. Fully measure the opposites ('hot, cold," "day," "night," etc.). This is what sets William Shakespeare apart from his contemporaries; the ability to infuse into his characters the complex and profound and deep by comparing what is to what is not.

6. Do not fear the words Shakespeare made up. The character is forced to speak them—to make them up *in the moment*—because they don't know what to say and yet still must speak! Also some homework will be necessary because the Bard does employ vernacular and slang that is more than 400 years old.

7. Experiment speaking the last line with an *upward* inflection, especially if it is a rhymed couplet. The last line is most often an exit line, and it is meant to proclaim to the audience that something tremendous is coming right up!

8. Write a sonnet. You will be amazed at how meticulous you become with Shakespeare's words, rhythm and meter after attempting to *write* like him!

9. Don't use a phony British accent. Truth be told, people in Shakespeare's time probably spoke more like the hill people of American Appalachia than Elizabethan England. Use your own voice, whatever it sounds like. Also remember this: what makes spoken Shakespeare sound 'classical' is the tremendous *need* of the characters, not some pretentious, high-falootin' British-speak!

10. Don't fear Shakespeare. *Love* him.

### Iambic Pentameter

The dreaded Blank Verse. The five feet of meter made up of two syllables per foot, which is the bane of existence for young actors first approaching Shakespeare. So much more can and should be said, but remember this: the five feet and the series of ten Un-Stressed followed by Stressed syllables approximate the *beat of the human heart,* and if you really start to measure how you talk to all of your friends every single day you will recognize your very own speech pattern as un-stressed and stressed. Imagine that! You speak Shakespearean verse every day of your life!

## Rhymed Couplets

Rhymed couplets in Shakespeare must be pointed up as a clue to the audience that something important is going to happen soon. This is particularly true of the couplet that ends a scene, which I have mentioned several times here. In addition think of the character speaking a couplet or other line of rhyming poetry as *intending to do so*; they know they are speaking poetry and are doing it for a reason! The difference between Shakespeare and the verse of Moliere is that the Bard most often uses them to frame the end or "cap" a scene. Which is why they are often called "capping couplets."

# *Your Appearance*

## Dress like a Professional

I mentioned this earlier but it bears repeating. Unless instructed otherwise, simply use common sense: neat and clean and respectful, like you are on a job interview. Which you *are.*

## Costume?

Since I have mentioned clothing again, I should say one other thing. Earlier of course I imparted the story about the desperate actress in the French maid's costume. It is true that the actor must never ever come to an audition in costume per se, *however* it is helpful if the actor wears clothing that is at least *evocative and suggestive* of the character they are auditioning for. Be very careful here. It is okay to wear a suit if you are auditioning for a man in big business, a simple shirt and slacks if for a cop on the beat, perhaps a shirt and *clean* jeans if a construction worker, a nice dress with a *minimal* amount of jewelry if for a lady of the upper class, etc. as long as these do not approach the *actual* character in the play you are auditioning for. If done right this can help the auditor to begin to *see* you in the role.

## Tattoos and Hair

Your body is your own to do with as you please. But consider this: in being an actor, particularly a stage actor, your most profound desire is to prove to a director who might hire you that you can become *anyone, anywhere, any time.* A visible tattoo screams aloud that you are hopelessly of and from the *present day.* Depending upon the concept of the production, this might get in the way of your classical performance. With piercings of the nose, brow and tongue you can simply remove them before the audition. In the case of body tattoos it might be you could squeak by if you have the kind which would only be visible if you were naked. Otherwise the full body make-up prospect is a nightmare. For film you can now rely upon technology to digitally erase tattoos, but this is probably going to be only if the director thinks you are worth the trouble of doing this and that will likely mean that you will have to be a star for them to consider it.

As far as hair color is concerned it too is your own so knock yourself out. Just remember once again that virtually any play before and even the 20th century-forward—with the possible exception of shows such as *Hair, Moonchildren, Godspell* or *Rocky Horror Show*—is going to require you to have conservative, traditional hair color. You also want to avoid odd hair color for the audition because it can actually get in the way of the auditor *seeing* you; anything out of the ordinary that might catch their eye can make it that much harder for them to concentrate on your work and your work alone.

## *The Cold and Prepared Read*

Clown
But I pray, can you read anything you see?
Romeo
Ay, if I know the letters and the language.
                    *--Romeo and Juliet*

This form of audition is what is known as a Call Back; the director has 'called you back' no doubt based on your earlier prepared monologue to see you up on your feet with other actors working on the script of the production. It can come in one of two forms; the prepared read and the cold read. The prepared of course is best; this will mean that you were likely submitted by an agent to the casting director and they have sent it to you specifically to look over and work on before you get there. The 'cold' read is much more challenging; at this type of audition you are called upon to read for a certain part in the play without being able to read it beforehand; you are picking up the script 'cold' and you are expected to make choices in the space of moments. This often is the case with smaller theater companies who are in New York on the fly for just a few quick days to cast and therefore need to make decisions quickly.

Either way, whether prepared or cold this is the *real* audition, for you can trust that you are genuinely being considered for casting. The director will be looking at you for a lot things—and not all of them good; they will be looking to compare your height, weight, and coloring to the other people who read your part and with the person reading with you. They will be looking for the impossible—the way the part *ought* to be done. They can't know this, of course, because they don't know how it must be done—that is what you are there for; to *tell* them how it ought to be done. How do you do this?  It helps if you have played the part before (it is a myth that a director won't want to hire you if you have previously played a role. Actually they will most likely LOVE you for it because you will provide them with that much *less work* they have to do trying to explain to you how to do it in an all-too-short rehearsal period. About 75 to 25% of the time this is the case, in favor of you having played a role before). If you have not played the part before this is where your *talent* comes in; this is where you get up there and show them what you can do!

How do you do this?  Here are some pointers:

1. Hold the script up to your standing eye-level. This is very technical of course but it will help you avoid constantly looking down at the text held at your waist, and hence allow you to keep your focus up and on your partner. Also another tip: nobody will mind if you highlight in yellow your words on the copied sides (so yes, a Hi-Liter is handy to have in your travel bag or briefcase).

2. You must make a split-second choice; you must go on an impulse and pick something to *fight for* from your scene partner and you must go for it like you have never gone for anything before. And remember: *Lovers* do this kind of fighting every single day!

3. *REALLY* listen! This was spoken of in great detail in Chapter 6 "Beats; That is, You Must *Change.*" You must listen to your partner—their words and their body and their eyes—and you must change accordingly! But not just to the meaning of what they say; listen to the *sense* of what they say. In other words, you must *play* the scene with them!

4. Go on *every* impulse. You may as well; this will prevent you from wondering after the audition is over what would have happened if you had made the other choice. Odds are you will not be penalized *because* of your choice; it just might be you aren't cast because of *not making* a choice.

5. You don't need to look at your scene partner *all* the time! I first mentioned this in Part One when talking about "Cheating Out." This is true in the audition reading as well as scene work in class. In a moment of reverie when telling a story or confessing some tragedy we look away from the person we are 'talking to' constantly because the memory is taking us back in time. Establish the 'person' at the proper focus point and then you are free to look 'away' from them *out front*, where the director can see you better. This is even true—perhaps especially so—in the audition room as well as on stage looking into the fourth wall.

# *Lastly, Casting*

## If You are Not Cast—Don't Take it Personally

Many years ago a director told me that if you don't get a part you must never take it personally because there are so many variables in the casting process that you will almost never hear what you want to hear if you asked them why they chose you. Much more often than you are aware the answer will be "you looked right," you "fit the person you read with," you "were the right height," or, "you were too fat," or you "weren't tall enough," or you are (yes this used to happen) "African American and I didn't want to go that way; it upsets the historical perspective of the piece." Except in the case of not being cast in a role you can credibly play because the director did not want to employ an actor of your race—which is of course *discrimination*—never take your lack of casting personally; the people you are auditioning for are professional but also just as frail and human and vulnerable as you are. In the end, unless they have an agenda or prejudice they don't have the time to be personal; they are trying to get their show up in just three and a half weeks! This is why you will help them immeasurably when you walk into the room showing them the spitting image of the type they are looking for!

## Color Blind Casting

In speaking about preparing to audition I spoke about the actor's consideration of 'Does the director/theatre company have anything for you?' in terms of casting opportunities. It must be admitted that there is another Type, wholly unto itself, separate from leading man, character man, ingénue and leading lady and this Type is the actor of color. Color, is, yes, a *type* as well. Sadly I can recall years ago this being a barrier if you were an actor of color seeking casting in language plays. It was always silent and almost never spoken out loud, but it existed. By 'language' plays I am speaking about all manner of pre 20th century works. Thanks to Joseph Papp and his New York Shakespeare Festival, for generations the casting of Shakespeare plays have been a different case when casting actors of color because his plays are, we now realize, much more about words and ideas rather than culture. But years ago it took a while for some theatre companies to join the twentieth century, resisting Actor's Equity Association's campaign of encouraging Non Traditional Casting. There are simply some directors who cannot see a black or brown or Asian face in drawing room comedies and plays of realism before 1900. Happily in this new millennium times have changed; we routinely see multi-racial casting in Shakespeare and also the great plays of the world theatre; we see an African American *Saint Joan,* an all-African American *Long Days' Journey into Night* and *Cat on a Hot Tin Roof (*or a production of *Cat* with an African American Big Daddy and otherwise Caucasian cast)*, a Chinese *Death of a Salesman* directed by Arthur Miller himself. As a matter of fact, with *Salesman* the roles of Charley and Bernard, for example, have increasingly become casting opportunities for actors of color: George C. Scott did it in his Off Broadway production in the 1970's, and I myself played Charley in a production done at Missouri Repertory Theatre many years ago. Women continue to be considered for roles not limited to gender, the most recent iteration of this being Prospero in *The Tempest* played as a woman (Helen Mirren's *Prospera*) and a recent Stratford Ontario Shakespeare Festival production of *Julius Caesar* in which the title role was played by a resident actress. *Romeo and Juliet* have long been cast biracial for obvious reasons and we have seen African American Cleopatras, Caesars and even Iagos.

However, realize that some plays that are written all one race can be a different matter. In these cases you must study the play closely. *A Raisin in the Sun* only works if the entire family is black; the play is about what happens to them because they are black. This is true of most of August Wilson's work. These plays are telling cultural stories in which race is *germane;* Equity's Non Traditional Casting Project is about roles in which the race of characters is *not* important, is not hinging on the plot. That is the difference to be aware of.

Because of all of this and all I have learned over the years, for our enlightenment of today I prefer not to use the term, "color *blind* casting." Though it is meant to indicate inclusiveness with the best of intentions, to me color *blind* suggests a circumstance of almost ignoring the very being of the person in front of you; a race is not only about color, it is about a *culture*. I would like to gently suggest we consider the term color *inclusive* casting; this takes into account the heritage of the actor and accepts it as *part of the role* they are playing. For instance I have a particular hankering to someday play both Hercule Poirot and Dr. Watson as *West Indian.* This would help to explain as well as herald the fact that they are a character of color in those period plays.

If you have seen some of the recent film remakes of *Bye Bye, Birdie, Cinderella* and *Annie* on the Disney Channel you will have been treated to a perfect rainbow of diverse, multi-racial, color *inclusive* casting, without even a thought to family parentage or siblings. I have to admit that at first glance this took even me a moment to get used to, but ultimately this is where the theatre was meant to go; an artistic labor of love that speaks to all people at all times and welcomes them wherever they come from and whoever they are. This is why I so much love the theatre; we know it is not real, we accept that it is built upon illusion. And with that illusion truly anything on earth is possible.

It is also why I have loved Shakespeare so much all my career; as you can see I could not find better quotes to preface each of my chapters. His words—and the dreams and ideas those words inspire in all of us—have always been greater to me than any petty question of color. To this I say, 'All Hail!'

## *Summary of Part Two*

1. *In a Soliloquy you are never speaking to yourself. You are fighting for something outside of yourself.*

2. *A monologue must be chosen from a role you would play right now.*

3. *You must embrace your Type in all monologue choices.*

4. *A monologue for theatre should be chosen from plays which you have the opportunity to read.*

5. *A monologue must have a beginning, middle and end.*

6. *Play the antithesis and the love in a monologue.*

# Conclusion

To show our simple skill,
That is the true beginning of our end.

*A Midsummer Night's Dream*

I hope this book has been of some use to you. I have tried my best to make the case that it is helpful for the actor to consider a play as an outrageous situation caused by love. In fighting to overcome the outrageous the actor's choices must be equally as outrageous, and in choosing the weapons for that fight—the active verb— it matters *how* you fight for your objective because this will determine how closely you might come to the experience of emotion. Doing so will also energize the actor's choices in both scene work and auditions and will spark their imagination, helping them to make bigger bolder choices that will serve both the material they are working on and themselves, ultimately making them more interesting and more hirable in theatrical productions.

I also have tried to say that even though emotion is where every play's story must go such emotion is ultimately unreliable to be sought directly because it is based in the unpredictable human heart; therefore the actor's task then must be about *doing* something rather than about *feeling* something, and it is through this doing that feeling, at least part of it, can be produced. This not only gets the actor's work done, it also helps to make the actor work in such a way that is *professional*, and that is what I wish for all of you. No matter how outrageous certain moments of your future monologues and scenes may become, I hope this most of all will stay with you.

I also hope I have convinced you that there is, for the actor, no such thing as going "over the top." Test me on this: I am convinced that at least 80% of what a young actor does in *thinking* they are 'doing too much' in a rehearsal is *just about right for their scene.* Observe someone doing it, try it out yourself and see.

While I do believe it is compelling if we see a human being caught up in an outrageous situation, the most important thing is that what we are seeing is about *love.* Even if we sometimes find ourselves barking like a dog.

*Exeunt*

# Appendix A

## ACTIVE VERBS

Here is a list of active verbs to help you fight for what you want in your scene. An even more extensive source is the book *ACTIONS, The Actors' Thesaurus,* listed in the Suggested Reading section of this book.

They all begin with "I WANT TO…"

| | | |
|---|---|---|
| win | crush | search |
| oppress | encourage | tyrannize |
| stop | assault | prepare |
| possess | qualify | ruin |
| enlighten | occupy | renounce |
| violate | annihilate | adore |
| chastise | smear | get even |
| warn | relinquish | join |
| overwhelm | revere | obtain |
| desecrate | reassure | embellish |
| filch | stress | bombard |
| contaminate | condense | adopt |
| suppress | debase | abscond |
| tolerate | belittle | contest |
| withhold | swallow | lambast |
| clash | shirk | shoulder |
| help | calm | evade |
| approve | seduce | soothe |
| withdraw | accept | ignite |
| stroke | retreat | hold |
| build | condole | retire |
| buy time | hurt | cajole |
| quit | condone | awaken |
| dictate | exonerate | accost |

mock

authorize

crave

sanction

destroy

indict

discover

match

flatter

incriminate

bag

patronize

encourage

sting

penetrate

implore

invigorate

engage

compete

melt

idolize

torture

recover

diminish

charm

commit

liberate

bestow

disarm

dabble

assimilate

bribe

surround

cling

attack

torment

victimize

boast

crush

taunt

accomplish

clinch

incite

complain

concur

coerce

praise

tax

trap

terrify

strengthen

slander

redeem

validate

elevate

execute

chaperone

thaw

lionize

chew

vindicate

urge

beguile

inflict

absolve

support

manipulate

entertain

devour

plague

overwhelm

postpone

judge

mangle

avoid

hook

inspire

collect

exploit

clutch

tease

squeal on

capture

bitch

reinforce

hurt

force

beseech

fortify

carry out

recoup

commiserate

exalt

pursue

probe

excite

deify

prosecute

white wash

disarm

dazzle

impersonate

purge

emancipate

seduce

appraise

abstain

disturb

dominate

rectify

loot

assault          drill            abuse
dissect          pilfer           grovel

# Appendix B

## Actor's Character Score

| Your Character's Name | Super Objective | Objective | Action | Obstacle |
|---|---|---|---|---|
| ___ | What you WANT in the life of *the Play.* ___ | What you WANT *scene by scene.* ___ | What you *DO* to get what you want. State as active verb. ___ | What stands in your way? ___ |

# Appendix C

## SUGGESTED READING

Here is a list of books where you can find monologues and scenes to work on for audition and class work. In addition I have selected plays and playwrights I believe you should know. I have chosen just a few from each; my hope is that your interest will be peaked and that you will keep reading. Also I have included a few books on technique I think will be helpful to you. *Bon Appétit!*

### MONOLOGUES
*The Actor's Book of Classical Monologues,* Stefan Rudnicki
*Shakespeare's Monologues for Men*, Dick Dotterer
*Shakespeare's Monologues for Women*, Dotterer
*Monologues from Moliere*, Dotterer
*Knaves, Knights, and Kings,* Dotterer
*Monologues for Men*, Kyle Donnelly
*Monologues for Women*, Kyle Donnelly

### SCENES
*Great Scenes from the World Theater,* Vol. 1 & 2, James L. Steffensen, Jr.
*Neil Simon Scenes,* Roger Karshner

### PLAYS
#### William Shakespeare
*The Complete Works*

#### Aristophanes
*Lysistrata, The Birds*

#### Sophocles
*Antigone, Oedipus the King, Oedipus at Colonus*

#### Euripides
*Medea, Trojan Women, The Bacchae, Electra*

# Moliere
*The Misanthrope, Tartuffe, The Imaginary Invalid, The Miser, The School for Wives, The Doctor in Spite of Himself*

# Oliver Goldsmith
*She Stoops to Conquer*

# Oscar Wilde
*The Importance of Being Earnest, An Ideal Husband, Lady Windermere's Fan, A Woman of No Importance*

# George Bernard Shaw
*Pygmalion, Major Barbara, Mrs. Warren's Profession, Misalliance, Arms and the Man, Caesar and Cleopatra*

# Anton Chekhov
*The Three Sisters, The Cherry Orchard, Uncle Vanya, The Seagull*

# Henrik Ibsen
*Peer Gynt, Hedda Gabler, A Doll's House, The Wild Duck, An Enemy of the People*

# Eugene O'Neill
*Desire Under the Elms, The Emperor Jones, Ah! Wilderness, A Moon for the Misbegotten, The Iceman Cometh, Long Days' Journey into Night*

# Tennessee Williams
*The Glass Menagerie, A Streetcar Named Desire, Cat on a Hot Tin Roof, The Night of the Iguana, Summer and Smoke*

# Arthur Miller
*All My Sons, Death of a Salesman, The Crucible*

# William Inge
*Bus Stop, Picnic, Come Back, Little Sheba*

## Clifford Odets
*Awake and Sing, Rocket to the Moon, Golden Boy, The Big Knife, The Country Girl*

## Samuel Beckett
*Waiting for Godot, Endgame, Krapp's Last Tape*

## Edward Albee
*Zoo Story, Who's Afraid of Virginia Woolf? The Goat, or Who is Sylvia?*

## Neil Simon
*Barefoot in the Park, The Odd Couple, Brighton Beach Memoirs*

## August Wilson
*Ma Rainey's Black Bottom, Fences, The Piano Lesson, Joe Turner's Come and Gone*

## Lorraine Hansberry
*A Raisin in the Sun*

## Suzan Lori-Parks
*Top Dog/Underdog, In the Blood*

## ACTING
*An Actor Prepares*, Konstantin Stanislavski
*The Stanislavski System*, Sonia Moore
*Actions: The Actor's Thesaurus,* Caldarone and Lloyd-Williams

## THE ACTING PROFESSION
*Acting Professionally*, Robert Cohen
*The Audition Process*, Bobby Funk

## VOICE
*The Use and Training of the Human Voice,* Arthur Lessac
*Freeing the Natural Voice*, Kristin Linklater

## LABAN
*Laban for Actors and Dancers*, Jean Newlove

# THEATRE BIOGRAPHY

*Letters from an Actor,* William Redfield
*Being an Actor,* Simon Callow
*The Fervent Years*, Harold Clurman
*Act One,* Moss Hart

# ON SHAKESPEARE

*Playing Shakespeare,* John Barton
*Shakespeare on Toast*, Ben Crystal

## ABOUT THE AUTHOR

Herb Parker is Associate Professor in the Division of Theatre and Dance in the Department of Communications with East Tennessee State University in Johnson City, Tennessee. An actor for more than 30 years, he has worked extensively in regional theatre, stock, on national tour and Off Broadway. He holds an MFA from Ohio University's Professional Actor Training Program and a BFA in Theatre Arts from Stephens College. He has also taught at Ohio University and the University of Wisconsin-Madison and he has conducted workshops with the Tennessee Theatre Association and Southeastern Theatre Conference. He is a Theater panelist with the Tennessee Arts Commission and is a Respondent with Kennedy Center American College Theatre Festival and also a member of their Region IV Selection Team. Mr. Parker is a proud member of Actors' Equity Association.

23657573R00112

Made in the USA
Middletown, DE
30 August 2015